Telekinesis

Development of Psychic Power for Beginners

(A Beginner's Step-by-step Guide to Developing Telekinesis)

Rudolph Aoki

Published By **John Kembrey**

Rudolph Aoki

Telekinesis: Development of Psychic Power for Beginners (A Beginner's Step-by-step Guide to Developing Telekinesis)

ISBN   978-1-77485-483-9

No part of this guidebook shall be reproduced in any form without permission in writing from the publisher except in the case of brief quotations embodied in critical articles or reviews.

Legal & Disclaimer

The information contained in this ebook is not designed to replace or take the place of any form of medicine or professional medical advice. The information in this ebook has been provided for educational & entertainment purposes only.

The information contained in this book has been compiled from sources deemed reliable, and it is accurate to the best of the Author's knowledge; however, the Author cannot guarantee its accuracy and validity and cannot be held liable for any errors or omissions. Changes are periodically made to this book. You must consult your doctor or get professional medical advice before using any of the suggested remedies, techniques, or information in this book.

Upon using the information contained in this book, you agree to hold harmless the Author from and against any damages, costs, and expenses, including any legal fees potentially resulting from the application of any of the information provided by this guide. This disclaimer applies to any damages or injury caused by the use and application, whether directly or indirectly, of any advice or information presented, whether for breach of contract, tort, negligence, personal injury, criminal intent, or under any other cause of action.

You agree to accept all risks of using the information presented inside this book. You need to consult a professional medical practitioner in order to ensure you are both able and healthy enough to participate in this program.

TABLE OF CONTENTS

Introduction

Since the dawn of time, humankind has always believed that they can perceive and feel or touch, regardless of whether or not they have always ignored the things that could not be observed in the direct sense. Perhaps the most reliable evidence to prove of this is the formulas and theories developed by the greatest minds in the world and who were subjected to some horrendous treatment to have their work acknowledged. The most famous example of this type of treatment is Galileo Galilei, the man who declared his belief that Earth does not lie at the central point of the universe and instead revolves around its center, within which lies the Sun. Galileo Galilei was almost executed for his statement!

We know that not just Earth but seven other planets orbit the sun. We have proof of this however for a man, it took the greater part of his life to prove that it was true. The world has changed, humanity has developed and now has advanced ways of proving things that were that were once thought impossible. However possibly because of an inherent terror of the unknown certain people have the same apprehension that runs through their spines at the mere mention of terms that are rarely explored by scientists like parapsychology and telepathy. They also have telekinesis, ESP or projections outside of the body. Even if something is not completely understood by humans isn't a reason to say that it isn't there.

Contrarily, take the atom, its particles electrons, protons, as well as other, smaller parts of the nature's "puzzle" that we can't see them with the naked eye, and some even require the most powerful of microscopes, while others are only theoretically proven to exist. And yet it is true that the ENTIRE world is made up of particles. The things that are not visible do not mean that it is inaccessible or unattainable, maybe it is just that we require more time to get used to it and examine it more deeply. What exactly is required with the relatively new field of parapsychology.

When we talk about parapsychology, two terms spring to the mind of the reader - Telekinesis and telepathy as the main instances of ESP (extrasensory perception) although there are many other types of "paranormal" behavior, or as some refer to it as ridiculing the idea of someone being able to alter anything other than his own thoughts with their mind. Telekinesis, however, proves the opposite.

Telekinesis is the ability of an individual to affect the physical world around him by using the force of thoughts or more accurately, his thoughts, as we'll see that telekinesis does not have to be an action that is voluntarily performed. With telekinesis, we are capable of moving objects which are objects of physical nature, without ever touching them with hand. The phenomenon was known to be present for quite a while long ago, however just recently has it been subjected to numerous tests to confirm its authenticity.

In the past, for many decades even, those who had the gift were ridiculed and ridiculed. They were always branded as frauds and cheaters. Because of this, some chose not to display their talents in public which meant that it was a mystery until after the WWII period, where both Americans and Russians began to conduct tests on those with telekinetic abilities to have an advantage during their battle against Cold War.

Chapter 1: What Exactly Is Telekinesis?

The history of telekinesis

Telekinesis also referred to as psychokinesis is the direct effect of the mind over any object that is physical, and without being able to detect any physical form of energy. In simple definition, telekinesis refers to the an act of removing or distorted object in the environment only through thoughts, and without physical contact with it. The term "telekinesis" first came to be created in 1890 by Russian psychologist Aleksander Aksakof (or Aksakov) who coined the term telekinesis to describe the phenomenon. It is which was derived from the Greek"tele" meaning distant and kinesis meaning movement.

The term"psychokinesis" was coined later in 1914 in 1914, by American journalist Henry Holt, and derived from the Greek psyche , which is a reference to soul or life, as well as the Greek word kinesis which means to move. The original meaning of the word however, was invented to describe the strange movements of objects which were originally believed to be ghosts of dead people or angels, demons or any other supernatural force. It appears that telekinesis has never really emerged from the mystery of supernatural.

The first studies on telekinesis suggested that there was an unidentified liquid within the human brain that could be capable, in certain conditions of leaving the mind and altering the physical world surrounding it. This theory, as held by people like Camille Flammarion, French astronomer and writer, as well as William Crookes, British chemist and physicist who was the first to develop vacuum tubes and creator of Crookes tubes and the Crookes tubes, was later to be challenged by psychic researcher Hereward Carrington who is a well-known researcher of psychic phenomena as well as a writer. Carrington argued that any kind of fluid was an idea, since there was no evidence to suggest its existence, nor has it ever been found.

Although the first documented reports of Telekinesis date way back into the nineteenth century, a few evidences that suggest the use of telekinesis long earlier than that, since the beginning of time. There are many tales of people who did what was considered to be miracles in the past and that can easily be explained as telekinesis.

Folklores from all of the ancient civilizations are filled with such tales. For instance, there is a debate that telekinesis is the force that the ancient Egyptians employed when they built pyramids or whether Moses actually employed one form of telekinesis or another to break up the Red sea in the time of the time of the exile from the Israelites. While the majority of these stories are most likely exaggerated, there remain those tales of the time written by some of the most famous personalities of their time and also events that were observed by more than one person, and sometimes by hundreds. These events, which are proven by history to have occurred but cannot be definitively understood or defined, remain on the edge of being attributed to "supernatural".

In the past although there were some experiments conducted around the turn into the 20th century, this technology was studied extensively after WWII and during the time that was the Cold War. Both Russians as well as Americans sought to develop an approach that could allow one of them to target or even attack one another without sending soldiers to the actual battlefield.

It was the time of "paranormal boom" and the rise of curiosity about PSI powers Telepathy, telekinesis and various other types of "paranormal" behaviour. A majority of the experiments are well-known and definitely the majority of the most convincing tests date from the time of this period. However, telekinesis continues to be extensively researched and remarkable results are recorded every year.

The mysterious nature of ESP and the phenomenon of telekinesis

All ESP actions, as discussed earlier, particularly telekinesis thoughtsography (the capability to display one's thoughts onto an undeveloped film roll) along with astral projection were at one time attributed to otherworldly beings such as ghosts, spirits , and demons. It took a long time to educated people to see more of these phenomena than they supposed to represent, in addition also to begin to connect the phenomena to the more "lively" world - and to the real. From the moment the initial tests began it became apparent that the minds of people, or their minds were the ones in charge of the situation. In the following years the phrase "mind over matter" was used to describe these events.

There's hardly anyone of us who hasn't had a glimpse of ESP. It could be a telepathic experience in which we know exactly what our counterpart has to say before opening his mouth or a precognition Deja vu phenomenon, where we are able to predict the sequence of events that occurred in a specific event and even an ESP experience in which we're, for example, in need of a certain object we are aware is far away only to we spot it right under our eyes like it has mysteriously moved into the area, there's no one on earth who can claim to have did not experience something that can be said to have been ESP. However, is this truly an incidental experience? According to psychic research the answer is no.

Two fundamental kinds of telekinesis have been identified, small-scale and large-scale. The first type known as Macro-PK (or Macro-TK) is popular with spectators because it is the only type of telekinesis which can be visible to eyes that are not blind. This is the type of telekinesis that has lead to numerous disputes throughout the past century, because this is by far the most fascinating type. There is a different kind of telekinesis that is not visible to the naked eye. And it's called Micro-TK. In contrast to Macro-TK the Micro-TK type triggers modifications in molecules, atoms, and subatomic particles. It is visible and can be measured only with specially designed equipment for scientists.

If a person is focused very intently on an object in order of moving it he's really trying to accomplish is telekinesis with a willing intention. The goal is to move the object so far that it can be observed through the naked eye. This means the goal is to trigger massive the phenomenon of telekinesis. However since research into the phenomenon began in the early 1990s, it has been extremely difficult to find people who can perform Macro-TK on their own. It is rare to find people with that level of control and determination required to be able to do telekinesis at any given day. Telekinesis remains an extremely rare thing, but an ability that is available to everyone. A few, lucky ones are able to nourish and develop it to the point where they have the ability to demonstrate it to the world and the vast majority are able to do it only occasionally and are not aware of what actually assisted them to "do it". It is the research subject for many research studies, and it's widely believed that, like we said that telekinesis is an unwilling process of the mind. When we say unwilling, it refers to the process occurs on a subconscious basis, in which the subject is not conscious of it and aren't actively trying to attain it. Studies have shown that telekinesis is more likely to be developed in teens in the period that is the most advanced in mental development as their brains are receiving numerous new signals each day and they are developing cognitive states that go beyond the capabilities of a child and toward the adult. Although studies indicate that everybody can benefit from an telekinetic effect the phenomenon is typically seen among teenagers or those who are developing the ability from the time they were teenagers. There are many cases reported that we'll see later , of people who have tried telekinesis willingly for a long time, sometimes for days and were only able to achieve it after they had decided to quit.

Chapter 2: Can Telekinesis Be Possible?? - The Quantum Physics Paradox

Researchers now believe that we utilize only 7 percent of our brain's capacity. Simply put it's like if we had a country that was the size of the whole US and only used and cultivated a portion of it, it would be just a fraction of that of Texas. This would leave nearly the entire nation and half of North American continent, unexplored. This is also true with our mind. It is believed that even the greatest of geniuses have never utilized more than 10-12 percent of their brain's capacity. It leaves around 90% of the territory that is unexplored. What happens beyond the conscious mind remains unanswered. There could be hidden powerhouses within the recesses of our brains?

Beyond the "ordinary" enhancements like the ability to think better, calculate more quickly or reading in just a glance, consider the other "extraordinary" capabilities the brain might have. What if we were able to actually alter things using your brains or imagine images into existence, lift off the ground, or alter the odds of a betting game? We can. Many of us have achieved the process Some may have to work hard at it, but it's feasible. There aren't any supernatural forces that are involved within any ESP phenomena. The entire phenomenon of ESP can be explained by taking an in-depth look at quantum physical science.

For example, even though the majority of ESP phenomena do not conform to the established laws of physics the fact that they are not is not mean they are impossible. Even if we don't know the mechanism behind something doesn't mean it isn't. Maybe we just must try harder to expand our knowledge and amend the knowledge we have about Physics so far.

Physics researchers often make the error of accepting things as they are, and then not examining the theories that have been proved to be valid in certain circumstances. This was the case when it came to one of the more well-known and well-known laws of the field of physics, Newton's law of gravity. We realize that Newton's law on gravity is only an approximate, and is a good one to a certain precision. For instance, we could detect the force between two objects having specific masses that are separated by a certain distance, using Newton's law however, the accuracy of the results decreases dramatically when we increase how far they are. We also know that Newton's law could be used to some extent in the field of matter as we understand it However, what happens if applying it to the dark universe which has been confirmed to exist, but not visible? The results aren't as satisfactory. There are many ways the way that a particle of common matter could deviate from gravity's laws and general relativity. One can only imagine how erroneous a particle of dark matter could be. Yet, no physicist at least none of us has ever come out as if he has all the knowledge there is to learn about the science of physics.

It is precisely quantum Physics that is both challenging while at the same time allows that ESP phenomena, particularly the phenomenon of telekinesis to be feasible and reasonable, and without any "supernatural" properties at all. This is because on the one hand quantum physics states it is only possible to have four forces that exist in the natural world: magnetism, gravity or electromagnetism as well as both weak and powerful nuclear forces. With the exception of the two last ones as they only exist on a subatomic scale as well as their range of smaller than a millimeter there are only two forces that are electromagnetism and gravity. So, in order for a mind to be capable of being able to, for instance bend a spoon it should be able either to produce an unknown force or one of the two.

Quantum physics when paired with biology indicates that the human brains are not capable of creating or retaining electromagnetism in this magnitude that would represent the one force powerful sufficient to trigger the bent spoon. So, we have only gravity's force which isn't that powerful an force. The neurons in our brains given their size are not able to produce more than 10-9 percent of its force that equals one trillionth the force produced by gravity. We also already know that gravity itself can make spoons bend, and certainly not an even weaker force. To summarize because the human mind doesn't produce any kind of force that is new and the force it does produce is fragile, the human brain is not capable of bend metal or any other method of interfering with the physical world. Is it?

However this quantum physics theory has a different one which states that everything that surrounds us as well as all objects and individuals, everything in a single word, is a wave. It would be very insensitive to try to explain the entire theory here, however, we will attempt to understand at a minimum the fundamentals of it.

There is a specific area of quantum physics referred to as wave mechanics. It is concerned with the wave properties of light as well as particles within an atom. Because all particles have characteristics that are similar to waves, it is logical that all matter is actually a wave-like structure. The principles of the "metaphysics of motion and space and the structure of waves in matter" explain the way in which matter as we understand exists inside space, as a wave that interacts with other particles within the surrounding space. We're there! Matter isn't a solid-state thing anymore. It exists as particles, however, rater is a wave with properties. In simple terms, this signifies that matter reacts to its surroundings through sending as well as receiving them. What's the significance? It may be the biggest theory that supports that ESP may be a possibility and particularly Telekinesis!

Everything that occurs in our minds triggers brain activity. The activity of the brain can be easily monitored and was long ago identified by brainwaves. Therefore, everything we experience and think about triggers some brain waves. Based on the above theory that everything we're aware of acts as waves and thus communicates to other waves it's almost impossible to assert that brain activity isn't causing it to alter shape and form, alter its shape, or even change direction. If waves react to each other and interact with other waves, then all we have be doing is "fine the tuning" the brain's activity and then adjust it to the right frequency to alter the wave of the subject or the object we wish to influence.

To sum up, at the quantum scale, everything is energy. In 1944, in his talk "The nature of matter" one of the greatest German physical scientists, Max Planck, said: "There is no matter as in the sense of. Matter is created and exists only through an external force that causes the atom's particle to vibrate and holds this tiny solar system that is the atom. We have to assume that in the force that is behind it the existence of an intelligent and conscious mind. This mind is the underlying matrix of everything that is." In the event that we consider the theory of expanding space that has been which has been going on from the very beginning time according to the latest science, this means that at one time the entire matter that currently exists on this planet as well as in the whole universe was once packed such a way that it was one particle. In keeping with that the First Law of Thermodynamics, when energy is not destroyed but instead changes forms, then at some time, we were all the same substance. While this issue has spread to hundreds of directions, there's an underlying connection. If, by producing thoughts, one is actually using electricity, and the whole universe is made up of energy both of these energies have to interact at some level. This is why telekinesis seems extremely plausible.

Chapter 3: A Theory Behind Telekiniesis

"TELEKINESIS (TK)": The capability of causing at a distance using brain-generated motive force the motion of energy or matter that includes or is exclusively gases, solids, liquids plasmas particles of matter or waves of energy or particles. "

PSYCHOKINESIS (PK) is the ability to create either from a distance or through physical contact using the power of the mind and imagination to cause the most massive movement or manipulation energy, material or even the events.

Psychokinesis originates from Greek words psyche which means soul or life and kinesis, meaning to move. Simply put, "psychic" energy that is able to move objects without the use of a physical force. Energy can be measured , however it isn't always possible to use eyesight and other senses to measure its value. Some believe that the universal life-force energy is channeled into physical power for moving things. The energy and the intent are the extremely effective. It can be seen as a flow of water in which one directs or controls the direction and/or speed or intensity. The energy required to move objects directly is related to the focal point of the mental energy.

The Body

"Telekinesis is a unique method of motion for objects that (the motion) is not in our physical world was created in a different world, referred to as"the "counter-world" (the"counter-world" is the other world which was referred to by religions as the world made up of spirit)."

Many of us know that there exist many dimensions and worlds and this makes some sense. In the multiple dimensions as well as the "counter-world" as previously mentioned it is where mystics, shamans monks, saints, saints and magic adepts perform their healing and work magic. In the present world, both are merged and we witness "miracles" like things appearing out of thin air disappearing, reappearing and appearing odd weather phenomena as well as animals, voices, and bizarre lights as well as numerous other phenomena.

Psychokinesis-PK and Telekinesis-TK are not just is applicable to everyday objects but also to the physical and the spiritual body that moves from one place to the next or travelling at any distance from one location to another.

Translocation - Bilocation

Two terms closely parallel and directly connects to PK and TK is translocation and bilocation. Translocation and bilocation "kinesis" or energy could clarify is the meaning of these terms and illustrates the "movement of consciousness energy".

Bilocation is described by someone who exists in two locations simultaneously. It is a projection of a physical double on earth. The energy is transferred into an actualized form by astral travel, or unconsciously as a someone who is dying.

Translocation is defined as being more multidimensional and is used to describe experiences that occur outside of our bodies as well as UFO's which originate from different dimensions than our ones we have. Translocation refers to the process of traveling through dimensions that go beyond the boundaries of space-time and becoming physical in the particular dimension. The view from which we see is from the same dimension. This can be the case for Ancient Beings as well as apparitions coming present here, their dimension to ours.

In any shamanic activity travelling to other realms can help you understand the way energy and consciousness move.

objects

Mental activity is believed to affect the ability of puberty: major life changes as well as stress, emotional growth and behavioral issues, including spiritual growth and stages. The brain is a complex energy network! The Physics and Consciousness web site it's clear that subatomic particles work in concert with other particles. Thought waves are powerful not just within "thinking and cognitive" but also as tangible energy that's moving, flowing , and functioning like water. Powerful stuff. It's the "mental power" that we release and controlling the flow of this universal energy into the physical world - things that move! Chi, Prana, the Chakras all play a vital function.

We can conclude the telekinetic force is a natural phenomenon and is based on the physical laws. If it's natural, then why can't everybody do it? It could be because of inborn genes, soul's purpose spiritual 'level' training, motivation and purpose, responsibility...we can only speculate.

It appears to be the general consensus that this power "seems to have been" natural in certain individuals through:

* still being within clarity

"Art of Being Aware"

* Being in the empty space of the mind

* Letting go of unresolved problems (mental things)

* Special capabilities

Also, this alters the mind's capacity, allowing one to open and attentive to the flow of universal energy. People also possess this capability to be more open and aware when a certain set is reached, and they are aware of the frequency of a specific niche, such as tuning to an radio station. It's all about focus, concentration and clear thoughts. It's also beneficial to use vivid images. It helps to "see" that the moving object, which is then directed your mind more powerfully towards the object.

"The energy that is the foundation of the telekinetic motive force is derived from the brain region and not from the hands and not from the body in its entirety. It will activate briefly, in a controlled on or off state through a mental trigger that is learned and needs a brief duration of metabolic recharge, with an increase in effect the longer the inactivation or rest duration. A headache may be an effect of numerous activations within one row."

Practice

There seem to be a myriad of aspects to "training" to develop this capability in the attempt to move floating objects, altering pendulums or other objects hanging or suspended, changing the direction of a compass and rolling pencils, bent spoons, and even using divining rods for Dowsing. Some people imagine a direct flow of energy directly to the object. Others transform into the object. Some may use hand movements to influence the energy. Some simply imagine movements. An excellent object to play using are the toys made of metal that are balanced on a pivot or on an underlying base. They are movable and perfect in balance, which reflect even the smallest movement. Pinwheels that kids play with could be great as well.

Everyone is capable of this skill. To be an bodybuilder or marathon runner, we must work on it and build up. It's a form of mental exercise. Be careful not to think about it as a serious exercise. As with meditation when you are trying to TRY, you're too focused on trying, not doing.

Everything is a field of energy that is energy condensed. It's possible to do this with practice, you can learn to develop the mind to achieve this skill, even in the event that it's not naturally inherent without any practicing.

It is apparent that moving objects can be a mark in spiritual development , and there are many trying to achieve it. Many see it as a way to say "look at what I can do". It is possible to ask yourself what the reason is. When you've accomplished moving objects, you'll be asking yourself ..."Now How did you do it?" Keep in mind that it's not all about achievement.

There is a reason to boost kinetic energy however none is as effective and lasting as being conscious of the energy in the air around you. Awareness of thoughts and intentions, as well as how energy changes and interacts with your environment is vital. The knowledge that there are many multiverses to discover expands the awareness of our own consciousness and helps us define our identity and the things we're all about.

The Kinesis family of terms refers to becoming aware of motion and manipulation of energy and matter from one location to the next whether in this or elsewhere. This is not the "power" of doing this but the awareness of the energetic interactions, regardless of space-time restrictions.

Chapter 4: The Power Of Visualization And The Mind Of The Mind

As we've learned Telekinesis is, in all likelihood possible, according to current science. How can it be attained? Why don't we just have the ability of moving things? It's true that telekinesis can be difficult to master since it is, as stated the fine tuning of the brain's waves, however it can be developed easily by sheer will and determination. Like a smoker who is active who wants to stop smoking for all, just has to tell him that he does not need cigarettes instead of exploring different products from the market as we have to convince ourselves that telekinesis is feasible, and then think about how to get it.

People can be prone to quick dismay when things don't take the direction they want them to. This is not the right way to go if one is planning to tackle the challenge of a new one such as the telekinesis. Instead of abandoning the task, one should to keep practicing and practicing until they are successful, and if problems aren't going your way, practice more. This type of self-initiative and self-confidence are the only way to get to the ultimate reward, which is the motion that an item makes.

There are a variety of methods available to help you master telekinesis. even though they're various, they all share one thing that they all share - each of them instructs you to utilize the power of visualization. For telekinesis that is concrete they instruct you to visualize the object that you want to influence and the method by that you want to alter the state of it. If you can focus your thoughts and direct your thought and focus on your thoughts, you'll be able to accomplish your goals. Imagine drinking a glass water, for example. Then, if you try to smoke a cigarette while holding it from a distance of just a few feet, you may be able to miss it. Why? Because water is dispersed throughout but only a small portion (if it is) will go towards the point you'd like it to travel over such an extended distance, and then is able to hit the target. However, if you use an water gun and then pour the liquid from the bottle and attempt to do it again and again, you're more likely to hit your target. Why? because the same body of water has now formed a narrow beam of water that is capable of moving faster, at greater distances, as well as reaching closer to the point at which it is pointing. Try to focus on your weapon! Be aware that this isn't a method that can guarantee a successful shot. Sometimes, it requires more than one attempt.

Sometimes, it requires more. If you shoot a cigarette with water pistols chances are you'll be fortunate to get one shot within 3, 5, or 10 shots. In telekinesis, it is likely to be more fortunate to get one hit in the range of 104 or 105 times. It's one hit in 100000 attempts! It's the same thing as writing a sentence it is necessary to try writing your first sentence several times and use lots of paper before you are able to write it flawlessly. But the satisfaction of the achievement of telekinesis can't be comparable to smoking a cigarette or writing the first sentence. It's the thing that makes it worthwhile!

In order to achieve the focus required to be able to perform feats such like telekinesis or other kind of ESP you must remove all other thoughts, and concentrate only those thoughts that relate to the objects that he is seeking to relocate. Like throwing the stone into the waters, waves are spread in perfect circles beginning at the point from which it is in the water however only when the it is left unaffected by the surface. If you, for example put sticks in the waters close to the spot where it is that you are throwing the stone weavings break off against the stick once they are close to the stick. Similar to when you throw a number of smaller stones. The waves of each will be altered when struck with the wave of the other. Therefore, you will understand that only when you are pure-minded you are able to concentrate your mind.

What it can do is provide you with the ability for "thinking clearly" that is to say and without interruption from outside influences or other thoughts within. Through visualization, you can make your mind focus on just one thought in mind and then subdue the rest to preserve the focus on that one image in place. What your mind does, in essence is behave as a painter with a canvas in front of him with a model the front of him. If you think of your mind as your painter and your brain the canvas you have to do is to make the models so "visible" before the artist as is possible so that he can be able be able to "paint" the model, that is to arrange it in the way the way he would like.

To help people achieve the state of telekinesis, visualization exercises are suggested on a regular basis. They are not required to last more than 5 minutes each day. If you look back over every minute of your day with different "wasteful" thoughts, such as inattention-deficient day-dreaming, which happens to nearly all of us, 5 minutes of peace and tranquility is a minimal price to pay for the potential benefits.

In telekinesis it is creating a picture of yourself doing what would like to do to an object. For instance, if you're trying to smash a pen that is set in a vertical position on the table you need to imagine not just the pen falling but also the entire process of shifting your hand towards the pen, then hitting it with the point of your finger, just enough that it falls down. The visualization should be realistic and not dreamy that is blurred images of you instead, but the exact image of your hands or yourself as you move towards your pen, and throwing it over.

However, this image should not be forced. What does it mean to be being forced? You should not let yourself feel disappointed if you fail to attain what you've hoped for immediately. Instead, change your vision every time to get the desired result. The focus should not be exclusively on the outcome. The visualization should be calm and normal in its flow of thoughtthat is free of any external influence. If, for instance, you visualize what you want to accomplish, but fail on your first or subsequent attempts do not give in to the feelings that you feel of despair, anger, or despair.

The feelings you experience create an atmosphere of negativity, that your thoughts, whether you realize the fact or not begin moving away from your visualization and instead towards your emotions. This is why you are feeling that your visualization isn't functioning, but instead, your thoughts at the subconscious level aren't necessarily in tune with you. In reality, the more you work and the more time you put into attempting to force your mind to visualize and the more determined you are to get the outcomes - the more likely you will be unsuccessful, because your mind is focused on getting results , and not to the proper visualization. More stress that you cause in your body, regardless of regardless of whether you realize it or not and the less confidence you've got and this is the reason you stop moving forward instead of showing improvement.

At the beginning, regardless of whether your visualization is appropriate or not, you'll probably have very only a little (if even) success. It is not due to the way you think, or how you visualize, and definitely nothing to do with having to be "special" sufficient. Although you may hear that only certain individuals can be telekinesthetic, that's not the case. ANYONE can achieve it, but it does require some time to practice. If you fail the first time it's all to do with how you think. If you're unfamiliar with the idea of visualization even if you follow each rule, and draw accurate images in your head but you need to be able to accept the concept of visualization in general.

Everyone is accustomed to having many thoughts circulating around our heads when we try to accomplish any task normally involves locating the appropriate one and, in a metaphorical sense by reciting it. In this case, you have to completely block out all other thoughts and amplify the one you want and keep it in a discrete manner, without imposing the result. The initial discomfort could be due to the fact that you're seeking to "invoke" is something that was always part of you, yet you've never had the chance to tap into it before. So, you should take a break and allow it to be part of your.

Repeatedly doing this will train your brain to ease itself into a state where it draws attention to desired items and makes them a part of your thoughts. In addition, since we've observed that the subconscious portion of the brain is generally the one in charge of telekinesis you aid the subconscious part of your brain "see" the data that you're presenting it to and it will to believe it more strongly.

If you follow the simple rules, you'll be amazed at your results. If you're persistent enough and have faith in yourself, you will achieve it. Do not be obstinate and just follow the normal pattern of your thoughts. At first, guide your thoughts along the way as they will guide you.

Case studies of the most renowned mediums

In contrast to the conventional notion that a medium is only someone who has the ability to connect with the spirit world from the deceased, they are anyone who can perform any of the abilities that can be described as ESP. The history of the world is filled with recorded and written stories of individuals and heroes who have achieved amazing feats like the ability to telepathically communicate, astral projection, or the phenomenon of telekinesis. These people can all be classified into medium. If you look an in-depth look at it you will discover that many of the most well-known accomplishments that were accomplished prior to the advent of the modern age and machines, which means that they existed long before their recording and certainly before we even knew about the feats, could only be explained through the telekinesis. As an example, as I mentioned previously, what is the story behind the pyramids? What was the method of carving the stones using the most basic of modern tools? And how did they get them to the location desired and then stacked one on top of one another? What about the fact that Moses actually break of the sea in order to ensure the safety to the Israelites?

There are countless other instances of these accomplishments throughout the years. It is important to keep in mind that a lot of these stories existed long before they were recorded and every narrator could alter the story as they liked until it took the way it was recorded. Some of them may be over-inflated or not completely true However, something has to be the source of their inspiration. It is also important to keep in mind that we don't actually know anything about telekinesis. One could only imagine what it was 2000-2000 years in the past. Most likely, any ESP phenomenon was viewed as supernatural as well, and in the light of the rise of religion, it would likely be considered to be as God's creation, and, later, Satan's work. If we can't be certain of the events of our past, we do have plenty of written or recordings from our recent history, from the period of the last 100 years.

Although telekinesis has been extensively studied over the past 100 years, particularly from post-WWII through the mid-'80s there hasn't been any research that is thorough enough to establish that there is no doubt that it exists in a scientific manner but no one has demonstrated that it doesn't. Because a lot of these tests were recorded and photographed and recorded, it's left for the general public to decide whether the human brain is capable of doing such amazing feats. According to the information accessible to the public of everything documented and tested scientifically to date, it is.

Here are a few examples of the most famous media and the results they were able to accomplish.

Stanislawa Tomczyk

Stanislawa Tomczyk was most likely among the best well-known mediums of the modern time. The medium was Polish spiritualist in the beginning of the 20th century. Although there aren't many images from this period, it is claimed that she had many talents that include Telekinesis (the documents written in the document state "producing movements that were not in contact") and stopping the movements of a clock that was displayed inside a glass container and altering the roulette table to set the numbers by her own more often than was just a matter of chance. It was believed that she caused the movement of these objects via the tiny threads that grew at the tips of her fingers during séances. These threads were extremely thin and, when cut into half by cutting tools, they were instantly restored to their original form. The threads were easily visible because the experiments typically were conducted in a bright lighting.

Photograph of Stanislawa Tomczyk taken in 1913, which depicts her floating with a pair of scissors suspended in mid-air. The hands of her

were examined and cleaned before every dance, but it was not possible to determine why she did it.

Tomczyk was under the supervision by the psychologist Julian Ochorowicz, who led the séances and controlled the surroundings they were working in in Wisla, Southern Poland. It was said that what Ochorowicz did was frequently hypnotize Tomczyk to help her heal What he discovered was she seemed to be manipulated by the spirit known as "Little Stasia" that, according to her self-described words, wasn't an entity from anyone who died. Later, he discovered the truth that Little Stasia is actually an abbreviation of Tomczyk's personal surname, Stanislawa, and that it was most likely her alter ego or double and therefore was a part of her. The truth was revealed in one instance when he managed to get an image of Stasia in a space without any light source, whereas Stanislawa was in a different room. Unfortunately, even with modern amazing technology like the internet the photo cannot be found.

In 1909 one of Tomczyk's séances was observed by professor Theodore Flournoy, who was amazed by the results and was left in himself: "... in no doubt of the fact of telekinesis that was simple. ....". The experiment was repeated a short years later, in Geneva, Switzerland, and was fluornoy's professors Clarapede Cellerier as well as Batelli, as well as Fluornoy's personal son. But, this time the audience members were disappointed.

Further research was conducted in 1910 by scientists from an experimental laboratory for physical science located in Warsaw, Poland, where Tomczyk achieved remarkable results in the rigors of testing. The results and the entire research were later presented by Baron Schrenck Notzing in his 1920 book "Physikalische Phenomene des Mediumismus".

Eusapia Palladino

Eusapia Palladino (21.01.1854 1854 - 16.05.1918) was an Italian medium well-known for her performances that she staged all over Europe that included France, Germany, Poland and Russia. The performances were not cheap in the era of her time but anyone who was able to afford them could enjoy a show. Palladino was an extremely multi-faceted medium and her abilities comprised of multiple forms of ESP. She was famous for her ability to levitate and even expanding herself. Her talents included apportioning flowers, making dead, generating spirits hands and faces from pieces of wet clay , and even levitated tables. One of her most memorable performances was when she played an instrument on the table, without physical contact. She also claimed to speak to dead people through the spirit guides of John King. She was recognized as a real talentand her followers comprised some of the most brilliant minds of our time as well as several Nobel Prize laureates.

Palladino is a native of Minervino Murge, Bari province, Italy, into a family of peasants. The fact that she was born in Bari province could have helped her career as she was regarded as to be a normal woman who had extraordinary abilities, which was in contrast to the prevailing belief that only mystics could do "miracles".

Eusepia Palladino at one of her séances

Of the many people who studied her accomplishments across Europe Perhaps the most famous are Nobel Prize laureates Charles Richet who studied her over many years. They also studied Pierre as well as Maria Curie and Jean Perrin and Jean Perrin, who studied her when she was conducting her séances in Paris. Pierre Curie was, in the absence of a better description impressed by her feats and later wrote about her seancesthat "It was fascinating, and in reality, the phenomena we observed seemed inexplicably illusions--tables elevated from all four legs, the moving of objects that were afar as well as hands that smack or touch you, or make dazzling appearances. In a set that we created with only a few viewers all of whom we knew and with no possibility of a third party. The only trick that is possible is one that results from the extraordinary ability of the magician as a medium. How do you explain the phenomenon when one is in the position of holding feet and hands, and the light is strong enough that one is able to see everything that is happening?"

As she aged, her abilities began to diminish and she began to perform less often, and ended up disappearing from the European public stage.

Swami Rama

A fascinating case that is worth noting could be that of that of an Indian holy man dubbed Swami Rama. The man was born on the 25th of May 1925, in a tiny village located in the northern part of India situated within the Himalayas of Garhwal. From the time when he was a child, the family was taken in and educated by his master Bengali Baba, who later convinced him to go to the West in the USA, where he spent the majority of his time teaching. He traveled across Europe as well as the USA.

Swami Rama is perhaps the most well-known of the Indian holy men because Swami Rama was the first one to let Western researchers to examine him as well as carry out tests on him in the 1960s. Before him , there was no holy person was permitted to be studied or even recorded when performing, most certainly not performed by western scientists or even Americans.

It was 1969 when the doctor. Elmer Greene and his wife got a call to Dr. Daniel Ferguson regarding a patient that he was treating at the time at the Veterans Administration Hospital in St. Paul, Minnesota. Doctor. Ferguson informed the couple that he had an peculiar person, one who could control the heartbeat of his own body and completely eliminating his pulse. Ferguson asked the couple to organize an scientific team to study and visit the Yogi. The couple was established and the experiment began.

Through these many experiments the yogi displayed diverse forms of what can be described as a control. In one test, Rama was able to increase the temperature on the left arm of his right hand by several degrees over the right arm without changing hands. What's unique about Rama's situation was that, in the case of this, and several other studies it was necessary to use a polygraph to verify if he is truly able to achieve the claim he made and did it on his own initiative. In fact, what the test on polygraphs revealed was that the tone of his voice while he announced the start of the experiment was synchronized with the beginning of the changes that were taking place inside the body.

Another fascinating, yet hazardous experiment was conducted the time Rama decided to stop his heartbeat and the blood flow for 17 seconds without blinking in order to demonstrate the presence of something unusual. The experiments also proved that Rama was able to generate different types of brain waves even sleep-related ones, while being conscious of the environment.

On two occasions, Swami Rama was able to move a knitting needle five feet away and was under strict supervision. In particular his mouth was protected with a specially-designed mask to ensure that he couldn't generate the necessary air to trick to manipulate the needle. His entire body was encased in an outfit. Additionally, all vents in the room were closed for purposes of the test. However, the physician who was in the room at that time wasn't convinced that the conditions were properly controlled which led to the suggestion that there could have been some sort circulation of air.

Swami Rama died in 1996. He is famous for establishing the Himalayan Institute for Yoga Sciences and Philosophy and is among the top well-known names in both Indian as well as parapsychology around the world. In the end, he stated that his abilities were due to the methods of meditation that he learned over years of study and only that.

Of the people who demonstrated in addition to the power of telekinesis the following three were the most famous mediums, the most thoroughly examined and their feats were documented in photographs and on tape. This is due to their status as among the most recently discovered "wonders". They've been the subject of many of the most heated debates about ESP However, they've never been proved in any way to be either fakes or genuine phenomena.

Ted Serios

Of the three well recognized psychics Ted Serios is probably the most unusual. The year 1918 was the birth of Ted Serios. Serios had been a Chicago Bellboy, who claimed to have been gifted with psychic abilities. However, his abilities were different from those of other people. In particular, what he was able to accomplish was different from other form of telekinesis it was very similar to what Chinese refer to as "Nensha" which is the ability to cut the thoughts of a person onto a surface. Serios was able of transferring the thoughts of his mind onto an undeveloped roll film. The technique he developed was called "thoughtography".

Ted believed that his visions were the result of his psychic powers however, his tales only received credibility after a psychiatrist from Denver, Jule Eisenbud (1908-1999) became interested in him and recognized Serios' work. Thanks to Eisenbud as his mentor, Serios was a worldwide sensation in just a few years.

Ted's work method was as follows:

He would pick an object of a small size which he explained was necessary to help him focus and then place it on the camera's lens. Once he was at the point of being prepared, he would give the signal to the photographer to open the shutter or take the initiative himself. The camera was usually pointed toward the forehead of his subject He was able to take some stunning photos. They ranged from pictures he'd seen all around him, to precise photographs of buildings from locations which he'd never been to. Sometimes, he was in a position to do these feats even at a distance of a few feet away distant from his camera.

A fascinating aspect of Serios can be that the photographer was usually drunk or intoxicated when taking his photographs. In the few instances when Serios wasn't drunk, the only photos the photos he could create photographs were "blackies" or "whities" according to what Eisenbud called these, which were mostly black or overexposed photos.

The images he took were clear and clearly illustrating an object or location that is able to be located. Because of this, some could be seen differently and it was therefore difficult to determine to determine if something different from blur was present in the images. However, the ones that were near perfect gave a somewhat blurred view of the real world. This was precisely what puzzled the scientists who worked with him. According to some in the case of dreams, our brain actually detects distortions in reality. The images projected in clear form showed precisely these features. Of the most well-known photos two stand out as particularly significant one is the image of the Eisenbud ranch, showing the barn that was out in the wrong place and different as well as the one of the entryway into the headquarters of the Canadian Royal Mounted Police, in which "CANADIAN" was written as "CAINADAIN".

Ted also demonstrated a small degree from an ESP phenomenon known as remote viewing. As part of the experiment volunteers were required to participate in the sessions, and to hold envelopes that contained images Ted was to reproduce. The report states that Ted was extremely successful in reproducing images that he had absolutely nothing about.

While he was, repeatedly accused of being a fraud, he did not admit to being a cheat or committing fraud, and no evidence was ever discovered to support the assertions.

Ted Serios, who in his final years was adamant about not drinking alcohol, died in the year 2006 aged 88.

Uri Geller

A man who demonstrated incredible success in several fields of ESP such as telekinesis and telepathy, Geller was born in 1946 in Tel Aviv, which was at the time the British Mandate of Palestine, Izrael. When he was a young boy of 11 Geller moves with his family Cyprus and attends the college and teaches English. As a model during 1968-69, Geller began playing for small audiences at nightclubs, as an entertainer and soon became well-known in Israel. In the following years, Geller started visiting public auditoriums, halls, and military bases , and doing his "miracles" using metal. It was his forte and was the basis of his professional career. What exactly is this amazing person can do?

In his own declarations, Uri Geller possessed the abilities of telekinesis, psychic telepathy, and Dowsing. His shows included, for instance bent spoons, as well as other objects made of metal, figuring out secret drawings and stopping watches, and moving the needle on the compass solely by the force of his thought. He was famous for his performances live on TV shows.

The most well-known Telekinetic talent was the ability to bend spoons. That is, Geller was exceptionally adapt to causing spoons, keys and other cutlery objects to bend by using the power in his subconscious. He would pick up a metal object, at first was held by him, but later on it was actually permitted to viewers, show host or guest to grip it, and then he would gently rub the surface of the object with one or two fingers like a gentle touch but never exerting any apparent force on it, and the object would begin to gradually be bending. Forks and spoons it was possible to "soften" the metal to the point that they eventually broke in half. It is possible to find a evidence-based case from one of his live television appearances, where he was able to cut a ladle that was held by the host the space of minutes. There are many these videos on the internet, demonstrating Uri's incredible ability. The powers of telepathy and telekinesis grew so large that people frequently reported having their keys or other metallic objects bent in their homes, when watching his shows and listening to his instructions.

Another aspect Geller can do and was also video-documented while his examination was taking place and analyzing his mental projection of the image or number onto another. He can project an image of what he was looking for into the mind of another and then provide the person with an item of paper on which to write or draw the image they were seeing. He could have another piece of paper that he had drawn with what is on it.

The idea was that it was predicted that the two would coincide. The thing he was famous for was the reversed procedure. In other words, he would have one person write on paper or draw something to hide it from eyes, perhaps putting the item in an envelope, or something similar and then make a guess or draw what he got. The drawings he made were nearly always the exact same as they were in the original. Even if they weren't exactly the same as that of the source, they contained a good 90% similarity. There is only one instance of him not having an image. It turned out to be his most abstract picture that he's ever drawn. Even that case can be considered missing only in terms of scientific research. If you're an untrained person the resemblance between them is astonishing. It is interesting to note that he had one thing in common with thought-maker Ted Serios. The majority of the drawings that he created from the images he received were mirror images of the actual drawing, or were altered in a small way however, never so enough to not be identifiable. Like with Serios the fact that this was discovered to be fascinating, since the humans' brains do experience the world as mirror images. In his television shows, Geller often performed this to entertain his audience and as stated, the majority of times he achieved remarkable outcomes.

In his first shows, and sometimes later in the future, Geller would make old watches work or completely stop them for a certain period of time. Also, after seeing his programs, many at home complained of seeing their old watches stop or begin to work again. Because of these feats and the "miracles" occurring to viewers who watched his shows from their homes, Geller acquired masses of viewers across the world, and gained scientific attention across the globe that decided to give greater at the young man who claimed claims to have psychic abilities. In December of 1972 scientists from the Stanford Research Institute, Menlo Park, California, conducted some experiments with Geller with his permission of course, to determine whether he was truly a medium or just a scam artist. The tests were carried out under controlled conditions and they were documented thoroughly in both written and video cassettes.

Uri Geller in one of the tests

In these experiments, Uri displayed all of his most well-known feats, but also proved that he had more tricks than he could have imagined. One of his experiments that a video of can be found on the internet, Geller exhibited strong dowsing capabilities when the task was to locate an iron bearing in one of the containers in twelve of these containers. They were "double blind" experimentsin which neither the scientist who was experimenting with Geller or Geller could determine the exact location of the correct container. A third party could rearrange the containers to accommodate them. Through these testing, Uri was able to perform exceptionally and initially had to examine the containers by hand and eliminate any that weren't right. Naturally, he was prohibited from touching any of them or it would be considered a failing. After the first experiments that were all successful, Geller reportedly got to the point that he no longer require a hand at all, or even went as far as he could point to the correct container simply by gazing at them when entering the room.

In a second "double blind" experiment, a dice was put in a box and then it was shuffled by another person. Geller was required to guess the number that appeared on the die with the face facing towards the upwards. While he only managed to get twice of the 10 total and all eight guesses were right. The chance for pure chance is around 1:1000000 and that's exactly what the researchers wanted to achieve.

There were several more tests conducted by Geller which we do not be able to mention here. He completed all of them with success However, ironically those that focused on the characteristic Geller was most famous for that of bending metal, even though they were carried out during tests and not recorded as a success, but instead was noted as "additional research required". This is because although Geller claimed to be capable of bending metal at the distance, he wasn't not able demonstrate it in the course of testing. He had to keep the objects in place to be able to bend them, which was considered not a success since he had the ability to directly affect the object.

However, the research conducted by the scientists Harold Puthoff and Russell Targ found that, so they both experts were concerned Geller displayed characteristics that remain unproven in the scientific method and could not be replicated in any other manner in a controlled atmosphere The two scientists declared that he was a real psychic. Of obviously there were those who weren't convinced, as is the case for all psychics, however it certainly assisted Geller's career and transformed his career into a television actor, who became a acquaintance to Michael Jackson and a very well-known figure in the all over. Geller even appeared in a few films in the '00s.

Geller in his car from 1976. Cadillac filled with pieces of cutlery that he had handed to him or touched by some of the most famous people in the history of mankind.

Of all the mediums listed in this article, Uri Geller is the only one that is still active. He's still around and has occasional shows. He's possibly the most debated media of the last few years however, even though plenty of controversy was made about his work and achievements however, nobody has ever proven that he was a fraud or hoaxer without any doubt.

Nina Kulagina

The most renowned medium of the present is Russian Nina Kulagina. Born in 1926, as Ninel Sergeyevna Kulagina in St. Petersburg, Russia, Kulagina was one of the most researched mediums of all time. In contrast to Geller who was only studied for a brief period, and the vast majority of video footage of him originates from his own shows or appearances on other videos, and photographs of Kulagina originate from studies she conducted by her. It is possible to declare that Kulagina was extensively studied throughout the course of her life. However, the majority of her experiments were carried out in her Cold War era when the competition against Russia and the US as well as Russian in a variety of areas was gaining momentum and many claimed that her achievements were component the Russian media, Kulagina remains the best known medium for study, since scientists from all over the globe and across every field of study were studying her, including Germans in addition to Americans. There were two Nobel Prize laureates.

As she describes it, Kulagina was aware of her abilities as a young girl when, at one point in her anger the objects started to move away from her every time she approached them. Then, other events began to happen in the apartment, including lights turning on and off, as well as items moving either away or toward her, and rearranging her apartment. She realized she was the one responsible for these phenomena, and she had psychic abilities. She learned how to manage these powers and activate these powers whenever she wanted.

In 1964, she experienced an emotional breakdown and was in the hospital. At the time, Nina did a lot of sewing, both for fun as well as to distract her away from the hospital. The doctors were astonished when they observed that she picked the exact color of thread she desired from the basket in which she stored the threads, and never looked in the bin. The doctors reached out to local parapsychologists who, after her recovery in the next year began conducting experiments with her. It appears that Kulagina was capable of "see" the color of the spectrum with her fingertips.

It was discovered that Nina Kulagina was as versatile as a psychic in the same way Geller was. Her abilities included in addition to moving small objects across tables and making not just a an compass needle, but the entire compass move according to her wishes. One of the major differences among Kulagina and Geller however it is the fact that Kulagina was adept at moving any kind of object, no matter what substance it was made of. Geller achieved the greatest results using steel, easily controlled by magnets. This is the reason the reason why people are hesitant to believe in his feats in the present. Kulagina's primary limitation was the size of the object since she was able to manipulate smaller objects. The thing that intrigued Russian scientists most, particularly during her time in the Cold War era, was another one of her skills.

In particular, Kulagina was apt at in influencing the heart beats. Contrary to Swami Rama who was able to use the power to alter his own temperature as well as his heart speed, Kulagina could easily influence the other's. In one study in the year 1970 she was presented with an actual frog and the objective was to stop or slow down its heart for a brief moment. After she had completed this task with ease, Russians began to wonder if they had a different kind of weapon in their arsenal. This weapon was capable, in the event of needing to strike at Americans from an insecure distance, and from behind the iron Curtain. They decided to investigate Kulagina more thoroughly to find out how far her capabilities extend and, in a different experiment they asked a subject to see his heart rate reduced. Kulagina nearly caused a cardiac death in the man and the experiment was halted. The results of this particular study like all other experiments were kept secret until they were became public during major deflections of prominent individuals from Russia to the US began. Some of the records can be accessible via the internet and other sources, however, nobody is aware of where the bulk of the documents are. The magnitude of her achievements is only imaginable because, in order for her to remain anonymous and keep her name secret, she had to for a long time to use the pseudonym Neyla Mikhailova.

From what remains of the written documents One particular article is fascinating. A well-known Czech scientist who is associated to Prague Military Institute Prague Military Institute, Dr. Zdenek Rejdak, published the following article in Czech Pravda:

"I went to visit the Kulagina family in the night of February 26 1968. The Mr. Blazek, an editor close friend of mine, was there as was a physician the Dr. J.S. Zverev and Dr. Sergeyev. Her husband, who is an engineer was there. Doctor. Zverev gave Mrs. Kulagina an extremely thorough physical exam. The tests using special instruments did not show any evidence whatsoever of magnets, or any other hidden object.

We inspected the table carefully and we also demanded Ms. Kulagina frequently to change her position at the table. We walked a compass through her body, table and chair with no results. I instructed for her hand washing. After that, she sat and turned the compass needle over 10 times. Then she turned the whole compass, its case as well as a matchbox, and twenty matches at a time. I put a cigarette in her. She also moved it with an instant. I then shredded it and found nothing in it. Between each test she was subsequently assessed by the doctor."

Not widely known to the people, Kulagina too had some traits that Ted Serios showed. While these have not been recorded or at the very least, the documents are not to be located, Kulagina reportedly was able to imprint the letters A and O on photo paper and occasionally, imprint the outline of images she saw. A truly amazing thing which was also reported but without evidence was the fact that she was able to develop psychically film that was not developed and seal it in an envelope.

Another little-known fact and the reason it has been around due to the fact that it was discovered by Kulagina, was that at times her clothing would catch flames due to the huge amount of energy that she created. In a show on television, towards the close of her life, she was able recreate this phenomenon of fire and cause an intense red patch that appeared on the arms of an European journalist.

One of the most interesting experiments, and again an odd one, however well-documented in the video is when she is shown an egg that is floating in a glass vessel filled by salted and saline water. Kulagina has managed in the video, at the least, at about 2 meters to break egg yolk and white and move the two in opposite sides in the glass container. While it's not evident in the portion which is readily accessible, it's been said that if she could focus enough, she could even return the egg to its original state.

The tasks Kulagina accomplished in the manner one could imagine, consumed an enormous amount of energy. Kulagina was reported to lose between 2 to 4 pounds per experiment, and required to spend a significant amount of time between her experiments. It was like she was using the body itself as a battery to generate power, however her battery was becoming exhausted. It usually takes about 3-4 hours for her to prepare for a. This is the reason why many experts believe that she could have been cheatingin spite of the fact she'd be examined thoroughly prior to each test. But, she was using the time to concentrate since, as she stated she required a an uncluttered mind, free of thoughts other than ones that were focused on the task at hand. During her experiments the blood pressure would drop below normal levels or rise to a new height and the evidence available illustrates that during certain tests her pulse could reach at 120 BMP and her blood pressure would exceed 220.

The impact of the constant experiments on her body ultimately reflected on her health and she was admitted to a hospital in late 1970s after suffering a near deathly heart attack. The doctor advised her to stay away from any experiments for a while and she did that. They would be done however, not in the way she did prior to her heart attack. At the time, another taped experiment took place, in which two German scientists visited her home without notice, and while the table was being set for dinner, she began shifting everything around the table. She would place smaller glasses in larger ones, and then move them without any aid , such as thread or other similar aids, and she would do the same with a table tennis ball. Scientists, needless to say, were awed. With time the actress became less able to perform and then stopped the performances completely. If she had been asked for one final time near the end in her career, she became in a state of disarray.

Nina Kulagina died in 1990 which marked the conclusion in the Cold War and the end of SSSR. Her name is ascribed to her for being the psychic the most studied and for whose work are the greatest amount of evidence documented in video. Although she faced a lot of criticism when the very first experiments began, Kulagina was never proven an imposter and until today nobody, whether either magician or not, is capable of replicating her tricks exactly as she carried them out.

Chapter 5: The Way To Build Your The Ability To Telekinesis In Your Own

For those who are determined to work towards developing their own telekinesis capabilities The most crucial thing to begin with is BELIEF. If one is completely committed to his goal, he'll achieve success. Anyone who is truly convinced of the work they do have the highest chance of getting their goals achieved as with everything that happens in your life. Disbelief, doubt and doubts are not going to get you anywhere. Also, having being too doubtful about one's capabilities could result in nothing. The first thing that every person requires is positive thoughts and a positive approach towards the goals they would like to achieve, and in cases of telekinesis, a huge amount of perseverance and the determination to keep trying. As we've observed before, telekinesis has an inherent capability of our mind, however, when we've never utilized it, then it will take lots of effort and time for us to "wake" the process. It is rare to find mediums that were able to alter things. The majority of them were aware of this at an early stage in their lives and then from that point on nurtured their gift. According to their own personal testimonials lots of meditative and visualization as well as psychological preparations as well as a steady practicing. The other important aspect to think about is why one would want to be able to use these powers. Telekinesis is not something that should be used only to have fun. One must stay aware of everything around him and rid the mind of any kind of self-centeredness. There are numerous tests that one can take to trigger the telekinesis process, but only a few ones will get discussed in this article. Keep in mind, however that these aren't essentials as each of us is unique in a way or the other, and so every person will take a different method of doing things. These exercises should be viewed as a guide instead of an instruction manual. Each individual is welcome to alter them in the way that he or prefers instead of following them blindly. What works for one person may not necessarily work for someone else.

The most crucial point is to not attempt to do the telekinesis technique, because you're likely to not succeed. Focus on trying to activate what you know is an aspect of your. Don't chase the outcomes, they are going to appear in time, and probably at the moment you least expected them. Some take days to achieve people, or weeks or even many years to others while some are never able to achieve it. The right understanding of the whole thing is the key to success.

Method 1: Small object

Before trying to influence the item in any other way one has to clear one's mind completely. You can take as long as is needed, it doesn't need to be 5 or 15 minutes. Once you're comfortable enough and you there are no thoughts in your head that are distracting you then grab something and put it in front of you in a desk or other flat surface. It can be anything you want however, for novices it is suggested to select a light, preferred a circular object, like pencils or similar items extended to the point that a tiny amount of force is enough to lower it. The object must be put before you, but not far enough to be able to be reached by hand, or be influenced by breath. Concentrate your focus on the object. Take a close look and picture the entirety of it. Make the picture from it within your imagination as exact as you can, which includes its shape, color its structure, the flaws they may have as well as the reflection light it has on it , and the other details it could include.

If you're unable to complete it the first time take a step back and examine it again. A clear and precise visualization is essential to success. When you are satisfied with your final visualization, you can open your eyes and focus your focus on the object once more. Now, try to imagine yourself being in a relationship of the objects. Think of it being a component of your and that you are an integral part of it. You ought to be able feel its form like it was yours, and at some point, this feeling will change to an emotional feeling that connects you to the object.

When the previous step has been completed Close your eyes once more. Remain in the unity of your emotions and visualize your body moving around the object. If you are happy with the picture you have created then open your eyes and test it. Pay attention to doing what you saw yourself doing just a few minutes ago. If you can move the object just little bit and you'll know that you're on the right path. Certain mediums are better to concentrate the energy they generate through their hands. Therefore, when you are unable to achieve it simply by watching the object, put you hands across both of its sides from an appropriate distance. Then, experiment with shifting your hands in different directions to help channel the energy in the correct direction.

If you're the first person to try this type of exercise the chances of failure are almost guaranteed. This is due to the fact that the untrained mind, the concept of focus and visualization is not well-known. You must educate your mind to think about what you want it to rather than simply random thoughts like you go about your day. Important to keep in mind is that you should not be discouraged by your efforts and instead think that you've just taken one step higher up the ladder to the secret to your brain. If you continue to work you will get there every step closer.

Method 2. Candle

If you are unable to do effectively the exercises described using the previous method there's an alternative. The focus and concentration parts are exactly the same as the first method. Instead of a small item, you must place a lit candles in front of you. It is essential to be in an area that is enclosed to do this, so you don't interfere with the flame. The candle should be left to burn for a few minutes so that the flame has time to become stable. Observe it constantly and concentrate on it while waiting for it to stop. If you are able, keep your mouth covered with your the hands of your hand or with a touchable handkerchief in order to keep your breathing out of the flame.

The goal of the exercise is to guide the flame in the direction you would like or, at the very least, alter its direction solely by the force of your own will.

After you've reached your desired concentration level, by imagining you are in a relationship with the flame, and then visualizing your body moving around the flame, you've attained the point at which you are at your most secure. This is when you must be able to see, and attempt to alter the direction that the flame is burning. In the beginning , there could be a few minor fluctuations however, as you progress you'll be able to move the flame but also hold it in the direction you want for a short period of time.

It is important to note that success is not assured in the first go You should continue trying until you get it. It's the most effective method of telekinesis, as flame is definitely lighter than pencils however, it does have several disadvantages. For instance, flames are more susceptible to being affected by any type of air circulation. Therefore, you must ensure that you have no windows open and no air circulation is in place. At first the candle must be placed in the open and later, you must place the candle in a closed container that has sufficient oxygen to ensure that the flame is kept burning like glass jars. It is essential to keep the container be transparent, but in the same way, using any container at all can make it more difficult for the power to get to the flame. To get the best results, this method, you must not use your hands as it could alter the results.

Method 3 - hanging an object

The focus part is essentially the same, you must pick any object of light and hang it with a thread, so that it can hang in a free manner and does not have any obstacles to either side. The process is basically similar to Method 1, however it gives greater freedom of movement for the object since it is able to go either way, or or at least horizontally. Try not to move it to the left or right however, but however you want to move it. You could, for instance, think of taking the object in your hands, and then attempt to move toward you, instead of moving it sideways. If you're not able to keep the image you have in your head of your tempering against the object, but can imagine yourself putting up with it out, you can focus on striking the object, and then moving it away from you.

If concentration alone doesn't perform, consider using your hands as well. The distance between your fingers and object must be taken into consideration. If you feel more at ease doing faster, sharper movements then the distance must be increased to ensure that the circulation of air due to the hand movements to not influence the object. If you're more comfortable with smaller and less tense hand actions, the distance needs to be less, but so as to not affect objects in any other way than what was intended. Telekinetic.

Numerous lab experiments have similar designs. They contain a pendulum of a type. The objectives of these experiments include either moving the pendulum that is stationary in motion, or stop it when it is moving.

The method 4 is the PSI wheel

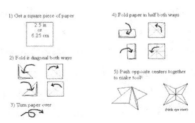

1) Get a square piece of paper

2) Fold it diagonal both ways

3) Turn paper over

4) Fold paper in half both ways

5) Push opposite centers together to make tool!

(birds eye view)

Paper

Needle

Holder

The most commonly used method, and consequently the most criticized by those who doubt It can be one of the most popular methods is Psi wheel. It is a simple experiment to do, and it requires less than a minute to make the materials. All you require is an elongated piece of foil or paper and a needle or toothpick for instance, as well as an eraser, bottle cap or an eraser.

Its paper (foil) is folded along one diagonal so that it forms the shape of a triangle. It is then folded and unfolded over the opposite. The process has to be repeated, but this folds the sheet in two halves. The result is a partially

74

folded paper which forms an interesting pyramid. The toothpick, or needle is inserted partially into an eraser, or a sponge, then the paper is placed over it in order to create a shape similar to an umbrella.

The goal to the test is for the papers to be moved in whatever direction or to cause it to the paper to turn. Also hand-held use is not recommended because even the heat that is normally produced by the human body may affect the results.

Chapter 6: Talking Telekinesis

What exactly is the term telekinesis? The word is derived from the Greek words meaning "mind" as well as "motion." It is at its highest

The most basic form of telekinesis, also referred to as psychokinesis (PK) is the ability to move objects by using your

mind. The strength of a person varies from to user based on their origins of abilities, their training,

age and age, etc. According to Bustle the character Eleven on the show "Stranger Things" is able to throw huge

objects can be thrown at electronic devices, they can turn them off and on, crack the glass and alter physical functions

Human beings and other beings. She is also able to access various dimensions, such as the Void as well as the Upside

Down -- that appear to be in a way overlap in time (and maybe space) in a sort of multiverse

configuration.

The limitation? The majority of telekinetics performing actions of mind over material is extremely taxing. Luke

Skywalker struggled to get his X-Wing from the Dagobah the swamp (though Yoda had no problem) and

Eleven is prone to nosebleeds when she pushes herself to the limit. The last time we saw "Stranger Things"

Gang, Eleven used her powers to block the gate that connects our universe to The Upside Down, trapping

the Mind Flayer, on the other side , and guarding Hawkins's residents. In its turn it is the Flayer

was watching from watching from its Upside Down domain, watching the Snow Ball dance and keeping an eye on the dancers

children who are a bit naughty.

Much of the show's story has focused on Eleven's personal growth following the Hawkins Lab breakout,

She's also shown significant change in her telekinetics, indicating that

Her powers don't stop there. Yes, they're the product of illegal CIA research and

sensory loss. However, the foundations are in place If Eleven was simply a small-screen

Simulacrum of powerful human beings that were hiding in time?

A An In-depth Background of Mind Magic Mind Magic

It's a spoiler: there's absolutely no scientific evidence to suggest that telekinetic powers actually exist. A quick Google search will reveal.

Find hundreds of videos on the internet However, they're not scientifically sound. quality to provide any kind of

substance. As pointed out by the neuroscience expert Mark Breedlove in a recent EarthSky article, the substance is

"Stranger Things" is a good representation of the 1980s fascination of the government with human mind-powers and the human mind,

Actual outcomes did not match those of the TV show. The evidence wasn't conclusively established to support

Telekinetic abilities.

Certain famous "telekinetics" such as Uri Geller have been praised through sleight-of-hand

illusions that replicate illusions to replicate mental powers, however it hasn't stopped telekinetic research completely. As

According to Live Science, researchers have switched their attention in the direction of "micro-PK," which can impact

microscopic objects or the outcomes in the course of time. However, these attempts have not been successful.

TheNext Level?

Maybe moving objects with our minds is not within our reach for now, but what happens the future?

Could the next phases of human evolution incorporate PK capabilities? From a biological point of view,

It's unlikely. There's nothing in our world to trigger this kind of change. We are the only species that can.

We aren't able to determine which genesor any genes -- could be governing Eleven-type power and are attempting to alter the genetic

Codes are illegal at best and highly risky at the worst.

It's not all negative news.

As reported by Psychology Today, technology could assist in the bridge between matter and mind through

Utilizing BCIs, also known as brain-computer interfaces (BCIs) to provide direct control of computers as well as other

connected devices that do not require to use voice or touch. Some of the efforts are focused on creating

Direct brain/device connections for treating conditions like paralysis or blindness, while other conditions have direct brain/device links to treat conditions such as blindness or paralysis.

creating solutions for thought-to-text that let users compose emails or texts instantly. No,

It's not quite Eleven shutting the doorway towards it being the Upside Down, but remember that she was the first to enter.

crushing Coke cans inside an hospital gown. Mind-meld emails may not be impressive but they could open the way for

the way to a new realm of telekinetic capabilities.

Learning the science behind Telekinesis

Have you ever been in a position where you're wishing that the traffic lights were on?

It will turn green and you are able to continue your journey or gaze longingly at a machine playing

To create an ideal match? It is possible that you should try again because you're able to create a match

which is accomplished through that telekinesis. Telekinesis is about being able to control motions of objects

through you mind's power. This is accomplished by projecting a portion of your consciousness onto the specific object you're looking to move.

The most common scenario is that you pay attention to the object, and you make it an integral part of your life, then

that you are capable of moving which you will be able to move. This is since you are at the point where you believe that you're

The third hand gives the power to move. The science behind it

will improve your chances of success in the field.

1. Understanding the significance and possibility of the telekinesis process is

Energy is the ability to work. Our bodies are brimming with energy that allows us to move around,

breathe or even work, or even. This energy comes through food and is also known as chemical

energy. There is only around 40% of the energy that is utilized for mechanical work. Cellular

the process of respiration releases chemical energy that is then used to create energy.

transformed into kinetic energy muscles. In telekinesis, the user uses the chemical body

stored within the body, instead of utilizing the energy potential of the chemicals.

While this chemical energy cannot be seen by an eye to see, it is there. The first law

The thermodynamics field states that it is impossible to make or destroy energy. However, it is

capable of being changed or transferred from one form that can be changed or transferred from one form to another. Energy that exists in all

System is continuous system is always in motion, and this applies to the surrounding environment too.

Contrary to what many believe Telekinesis isn't magic. It's all about the transfer of energy from

the body of one's, which is the surrounding area in this instance of an object. This is considered to be the body's system

as it is outside the object.

2. Feel the flow of energy through your body.

Telekinesis is a mental state that the object that you're seeking to control are just one.

This is why you must to feel it during the moment you feel the connection. It runs through your

body. Try two exercises to test your. You can stretch your arms forward and then stretch your arms.

each muscle you have. This can be done for around 10 seconds. you can do it in your first attempt.

too. In 10 second intervals, stretch your arm completely , and then try to feel the sensation of warmth that is passing

Through it.

You might be experiencing something that resembles an electrical sensing, or the temperature could be pulsating. What do you feel?

the sensation you feel when your muscles contract is the energy that we are feeling after your muscle contracting is the energy we are referring to. The goal, then, is to

The ability to manage this energy , without any type of trigger, like the trigger needed to shift your

muscles. Once you've reached the point that you are competent to do this, you can move on to

Learning to conserve ability to sustain the.

Another thing you can do is searching for a suitable cool area in which you are able to completely unwind

Your body. You can lie or sit so that your hair on your body do not droop.

This practice will require you to master the energy that you experience as natural, and to try to

Provide you with warmth to prevent your body from getting cold.

When you are able to control this, you'll be able to control the energy that is pumped into

insignificant things. As time passes, you'll learn how to transmit this energy from one region of your body to another.

other, like your chest or hand when needed.

3. specific about your method to manipulate the system.

Because you will be influencing the system, it's essential to be clear about what you want to accomplish.

to accomplish to do. This is in relation to whether you're thinking of pulling, pushing or spinning the wheel.

It is simple pulling the device up due because you be aware of where energy flows. However,

Levitation is extremely difficult as it is a matter of reducing the force the systems are able to absorb to be able to

so that it is light in order to facilitate the interaction of electromagnetism in the system and the environment around it.

If you wish to change the structure of the system, you have to change the entire kinetic energy

It is present in the system which is often referred to as heat. The quantity of heat

the energy needed to modify the system is measured as calories that is the equivalent of

To

4.184 joules. This is why it might be quite difficult to alter the shape of an object

however, it is likely.

4. Send the energy to their system

If you're able to harness the energy, you have to direct it towards the system of your choice. How you do this is entirely up to you.

This is because there are various methods that work for different individuals. Human beings

Think differently, and as Telekinesis is about manipulating the mind with objects and objects, then

You must find out what method works best for you. Prior to getting there, it's essential

to feel

the system and attempt to determine its mass, calculate the amount of energy required to be physically

It will move. Once you have done that, test to see if you are able to achieve the same level of energy to the one you

Feel inside your body, but even if you're not physically near the thing.

The most important thing to remember is the fact that it needs an ongoing flux of energy. The moment you realize it,

When you begin the process of changing the system, don't let it stop. Concentrate your attention on it,

or else, it will return to the state it was in, as per Newton's initial law which means

That something is at rest until an external force forces it. That force could be you.

If you are practicing telekinesis, then you must be aware that if you concentrate on long periods of time, your body will be unable to cope.

is exhausting and exhausting that can lead to occasional headaches that are mild every occasionally. However, headaches aren't common, they

They aren't serious, but they are a sign that you need to get some rest. In the past, it was those who

One of the most famous telekinetic performers to have been recorded talents the most telekinetic talent was Nina Kulagina who was a Russian housewife.

But even this powerful woman was able to cause objects to roll and shift but she was not able to make them move fully

levitate.

Telekinesis allows you to be capable of manipulating objects various ways, but that doesn't mean you're able to manipulate objects in a specific way.

that you'll be able to accomplish many impossible things spoken about as telekinesis since you will be able to do a lot of

They are just illusions.

Preparing for the performance Telekinesis

Telekinesis is a subject to doubt for many years. A majority of the time people don't think about it due to

in the sense that they are essential exercises to learn the art of telekinesis, regardless of whether it's related to your own or objects in your vicinity. The exercises you're required to complete will not benefit you the ability to control your surroundings or

Results aren't as effective aren't backed up with techniques results, and this is where visualization results come in. It can be used to improve

similar to meditation in that you first imagine the desired result in your mind and later

We would like them to be a reality and make it happen.

If you're ready to begin visualization, you should begin by working with very small items. Keep your eyes on

every tiny aspect, and this could be a matter of feeling, smelling or observing the color or even tasting

Then you'll reach the point at which you can see the whole scene.

1. Practice your visualization skills

Visualization is among the most essential exercises to master telekinesis, regardless of whether it is

It is about you or the objects that surround you. The exercises you're required to complete are not about you or the objects around you.

You will not see results , but you can't be able to back them up with the right skills This is where visualization can help. It

It works the same way as meditation, in the sense that you initially observe the desired outcome in your

in your mind. Then, wish for that they happen, and then work towards the idea.

If you're ready to start visualization, you should begin by working with small objects. Keep your eyes on

each and every little aspect, and this could involve smelling, feeling or observing the color or even the taste

These objects until you reach the point at which you can be able to see the whole scene.

2. Meditate

Anyone with knowledge of Telekinesis is aware that meditation is the most important factor in the development of your superhuman abilities.

skills. Your brain must be completely clear in order to harness the energy required

to manage your surroundings. You must not be thinking of other thoughts that could cause disruption or even impede

keep you distracted to get enough energy to focus on the objects you'd like to control. The

the fastest way to develop the ability is to practice meditation. A lot of people believe that listening to

Music in meditation aids the mind to concentrate, however it is not the case.

We live extremely busy lives and the only thing you need to accomplish to be noticed is to be juggling a variety of

Things at the same time. Meditation is a wonderful method to get away from all the hustle and bustle

that are connected to this kind of existence. This is where your mental process is triggered.

3.   Let   your   mind   wander
"$$$$$$$$$$$$$$$$$$$

The practice of telekinesis is similar to hypnosis, in that you'll never achieve the outcomes you want.

What do you want to achieve when you have an uninvolved mind. What you imagine is the outcome in the future, and that's why you'd like to control your thoughts, you'll be in the same situation.

If you do, you may believe it. The trick is to disregard what others say and do it anyway.

you've got. If you aren't sure you can be confident that nothing will occur. But you can be sure that if

If you believe in it, then there is no guarantee that it will happen, but there's a good chance it'll take place.

4. Be patient n

The importance of patience is when it comes to studying telekinesis. When you examine the background of telekinesis it

It took a lot of time and effort to perfect this practice. It is impossible to predict the exact moment you'll be able to master it.

You will be able to achieve that magic combination of energy. What you need to practice to. This is how you

It is not the same as losing weight, which is a process that shows results slowly. In this case, you must persevere

practice until the day that it happens, but you can't predict when it will happen.

5. Relax

Relaxing shouldn't be an issue when you're skilled at meditation as you've learned to

You can channel the energy that you require to perform the process of telekinesis. Imagine a situation where you're trying to

You can channel your energy, however you're focused on your work or your relationship or other issue. It can

This isn't possible, therefore the best option is to just relax. Relax and enjoy the moment and try not to

let your brain go away.

One of the best ways to get free of the stress we encounter in daily life is through yoga. Aside

From yoga and meditation from meditation and yoga, you can also take on a variety of exercises. It is essential to make time

the time to yourself each day in order to unwind. It isn't necessary to set aside much time for this,

approximately 15 minutes is sufficient for a few minutes and you'll see how much your days will improve.

If you are using Telekinesis, it is important to put aside the belief that you are doing telekinesis on is the object that you are

You are trying to control something that is different from yours. The concept is that you are trying to control

same energy. When you think that the object you're trying to manipulate is part of your being,

Then you will be capable of moving the item.

The art of learning how to perform Telekinesis

There's no evidence to suggest that telekinesis is real or can be taught, there's no harm in doing a test. If

You want to discover what you can, practice meditation to control your mind and then practice visualization

objects. When you are able to focus your mind and imagine the object's entire details concentrate on the object.

Connection to the object. Focus on the way you'd like to see the object expand and move.

The intention is to get the object. It is important to practice and so be patient, and continue to refine your

capabilities everyday.

Concentrating Your Thoughts

Believe that telekinesis can be achieved. It's unlikely to yield any outcomes if you try to do it.

Telekinesis when you have an unreceptive, closed mind. If you believe that there is no way to achieve this, you'll

You can prove your point prove yourself right, even at an unconscious level. Then, your goal is to

Make yourself believe that it is possible to move objects using your mind.

There is no scientific proof of the phenomenon, however, there's no definitive evidence that it isn't there,

either.

Daily practice meditation to increase the discipline of your mind. Wear loose clothing, and relax in a comfy

Position yourself in a relaxed position, then place your head in a comfortable position, and then close your eyes. Relax your body and breathe deep as you count to 4, and hold your breath for the duration of a

Four-count, and then count up to 8 while exhaling. Pay attention to your thoughts as you regulate your breathing.

Imagine that every thought is like a star in sky.

When you exhale, think of the stars disperse, save for one sun that becomes larger and

brighter. Moving, thoughts sluggish as your thoughts focus on the bright star that is.

Maintain control of your breathing and focus, without straining, on focusing your attention on an

One thought. People are used of doing fifty things at a time and are not patient. So, take your time. It could take a while

It is time to improve your mind's skills and focus your attention on one idea.

Try visualizing objects in the most detail you can. Begin by looking at an object in a tiny size

Around you, for example, an apple or a cup. Make a point of committing all of its characteristics to your mental memory. Once you've done that,

You feel like you know and comprehend the object, close your eyes and visualize the object in your brain's eyes as

As clearly as you can.

Make an effort to imagine the shape of it, its color and how soft or hard it is, the scent and other details.

details. Try visualizing while you meditate Control your breathing, focus your mind and concentrate

On a single object.

When you're ready, begin to visualize more complicated objects gradually. Gradually increase the complexity until you're able to

imagine complete scenes, for example, your living room. Imagine yourself sitting in the middle of all of the furniture as

It is clear that this is possible.

Be patient and continue working on your technique. Telekinesis demands that you be completely and fully present

moment. Your mind won't wander and your thoughts won't wander. This takes time and effort to attain this level.

Mental discipline is a must, so start daily meditation and visualization. each day.

As you get more practice, you will be able to get your mind clear and concentrate your

focus, and clearly see focus, and clearly visualize objects. Once you've learned to focus your brain, you can focus on gaining

Out to objects using your mind.

Reaching out towards an object

Focus on a small object, and only that. Set a small object in front of you such as a pencil or matchstick.

In the front of your eyes. Relax your mind and enter the zone. Be quiet and let the random thoughts, racing

Your thoughts, and you can be able to see clearly the object by using your brain's eye.

Make sure you are aware of the relationship between you and the object. Once you've mastered controlling your thoughts, and

Visualize objects, focus on the energy that connects you to the world outside. Imagine the

Matter and energy that flow through you, other objects and in the space between. Look for the boundaries

The distance between you and the objects around you disappear, and you realise that the object and you and the object are part of one system.

This is the principle that lies at the heart of Telekinesis. You along with the other object form the same. Try to move it.

You must be able to train yourself to believe this.

Imagine clearly how you would like to work with the object. Consider exactly how you would like the object to work.

move. Choose whether you want to push, pull, or rotate it. Focus on the object and observe it.

Moving as you planned with your eyes.

Imagine a single movement only. Do not get lost in the process or imagine the motion moving in different ways.

Concentrate on one thing at a time.

Your focus should be towards the subject. Keep your eyes fixed on the object and then send your message to it.

You would do the same with have your leg or arm. Make sure that you don't wander off and keep your concentrate on one thing.

The object is one of you. Therefore, move it the same way as the rest of your body. Don't get

Be discouraged when your first attempts don't get discouraged when your first efforts fail. Continue to work on discipline your mind, and

Try refining your skills with the use of telekinetic exercises.

Training with Telekinetics

Try to feel the energy flowing across your entire body. Stretch every muscle in one arm from

Your shoulder should be pressed against your fist for 10 to 15 seconds. Then fully relax your arm. Note how it feels.

Feels like you are building energy to build it, control it, and let it go. Make use of these feelings to enhance your abilities to

apply force to the object, and move it according to your intent.

Because the primary reason for Telekinesis is to feel that you and the object one, it is essential to feel and feel

learn about the energy that makes up the connection. Try spinning a Psi wheel. A psi wheel can be described as an example of a

The paper is folded in a pyramid shape which rests on a toothpick that is attached to a foil piece. The focus

The object is in your hands, so grasp it with your mind, then turn it around in your mind.

Simply spinning the wheel without damaging it will aid you in learning to control your

abilities. Put a glass jar, or other container on top of the wheel to stop wind from spinning the wheel.

Moving objects with psi balls. Psi balls are mass of force that is able to be touched, felt and even,

As time passes, you will be able to manipulate with your hands to manipulate objects. By putting your hands in your stomach and feel the energy rise at

Your core. Your hands should be as if they're playing with a ball, then think about the details.

Look at the ball using your eyes. What size is it? Are there any radiating areas? What hue is it? After you've

Once you have established the shape alter its form, move it around, and let it alter form and size. Once you have it, you can utilize this

ball to transfer the energy needed to objects. In the same way that it would be a baseball to smash a vase, make use of the ball to deliver energy to other objects.

ball can affect the solid the surface, or visible objects.

Controlling a flame is a skill you can master. Light the candle, unblock your thoughts and let the flame fill your mind.

Begin to watch it flicker and then move. While focusing on it then move it using your full energy. It should be moved right, and then it left,

Make it stretch to increase the intensity, then make it dimmer.

Alternate your exercise routine. To keep your workouts fresh you can try 2-3 exercises a day. Begin with

Meditating and visualizing your way to be in the meditation and visualization to get into the. Try spinning a psi-wheel or doing flamework.

Bending a fork or spoon and rolling the pen pencil. A variety of exercises can assist

help you practice without getting bored or stressed. Make sure you do each exercise for approximately

20 minutes, and then practice for approximately an hour per day.

You should stop when you're physically and mentally tired. Similar to any other type exercising, this is crucial to keep it up.

Take a break whenever you're exhausted. Take a break, eat a snack, drink some water and relax for a couple of hours. Find

return to work only after you're feeling rejuvenated. You'll have a hard time in staying focused if try to

Keep going when you require to take a break. In addition, you could end in headaches!

Do you do flamework?

Other than working with small objects, you can also work using fire. Consider lighting a candle, and

be aware of the flame's glow. Then, you have to calm your mind and then fill it by the fire.

Take a look at your flame's flickering, and apply your force to push it around. You can try using it to move it.

Right right, making it larger as well as dimmer, then you can you can make it do anything you'd like

With your mind. You can even dance.

The practice of using flames is advised initially because they are much easier to manipulate because of the

The fact is that they're not heavy objects, but rather balls of energy. Therefore, they will not put up a lot of a fight.

fight.

This workout is great for those who are exhausted and looking for an exercise that will help you.

When you start telekinesis, you'll be able to.

Try for astral projection

This is simply referring to out of bodyexperiences. It is an event in which your soul leaves

Your body is transported to an astral level. In order to be able to do this, you have to be in a deep state of hypnosis. Once your body is in an state called "vibration," your soul leaves your body to enter

the world all around the world around.

Although it sounds easy however, it is actually challenging to accomplish. It is recommended to begin with by making small steps.

for you to avoid to avoid. Try using your leg or arm and then feel the

out-of-limb- experience. Following that, you'll be able to move your whole self and also

Explore the various rooms before moving take a deep dive into the ambience. This idea could be extremely

Scary it can be, but you shouldn't give in to fear. Instead, let yourself relax and you'll be able to return in touch with your body.

Stop when you are exhausted

The exercises may wear you out, particularly when you're not getting enough time to rest. When you feel tired or depressed.

you're exhausted, either physically or mentally, take enough rest, and make sure that you do not continue

When fatigue wears off, you're getting back to regular. You'll be able to perform better when

You feel rejuvenated. It is the most effective way to tell whether you're up for the workouts is to pay attention to how you feel like.

Your body and your mind will tell that to.

Learn Telekinesis in just 5 minutes

If you are wondering how to master telekinesis within 5 minutes, or how to master the art of telekinesis in a day, then you must

We all know that this isn't feasible to learn psychokinesis. you require patience and time. The other will

surprised if they possess a remarkable abilities to manage things and exert power. Telekinesis is the

ability to move objects by using the mind. It isn't a physical method of control.

the objects. We've heard a lot of stories on the internet regarding this psychic talent. But not this one.

All the information and events are authentic. In the modern age the practice of making and distributing false information is not an option.

a tedious task.

Before you go through any psychokinesis video or images, ensure that it's real or not.

not. Look for the source on the internet. If you are confident in the process, then give it a go to test TKS. If you succeed, then take it to the next level.

If you failed the first time Then check to see if you followed the correct method of learning. Or else find

is the most effective option for learning to be successful.

A lot of people think that TKS is just about moving objects. However, in reality that it's about

studying the objects, their size, density and features, capacities as well as their colors.

Telekinesis learning steps:

If someone is interested to try psychokinesis is required to follow some easy mind-set steps to achieve it better.

1. Keep your eyes on the prize

Keep your focus on each mind-training session you've done. Concentration is the most important component of every

An excellent outcome. You should give some time and space to allow your brain to focus on the work you want to do.

A meditation practice that eliminates all distractions can help you stay focused.

2. Increase the power of concentration

To boost your concentration it is necessary to do various psychokinesis exercises. The

The best exercise for concentration will yield the best results. Keep a dot on the paper and hold it there.

Some distance.

Focus on the dot with no deviation. Breathe deeply and keep your eyes on the dot. your thoughts

Simply focus at the point. Remove all variations as you focus. You will be focusing more

more than five minutes in a row is quite a long time. But, one must concentrate on at a minimum

toward the end.

3. Psychokinesis can be learned through groupwork

Always strive to be part of an encouraging group even if you're tired. Group work often helps to

Increase your speed and abilities. Your coworkers could point out your weaknesses and areas of weakness. you are weak.

You can pinpoint the perfect opportunity to make improvements.

4. Freedom of Mind

The psychokinesis can only be effective with a clear mind with no other thoughts. The

People who are interested can attempt at least once a week to reach their objectives. Imagine is an essential component in the process.

as far as telekinesis is concerned. Simply imagine it and place the image to your mind and whatever else you're doing will do. It will assist you in reaching your core while doing telekinesis.

When you practice to reach your goal, make sure you follow your goal. If you haven't succeeded, don't despair.

If you feel that the object has moved, don't get angry; just continue learning the telekinesis exercises and be patient. Wash

Get rid of all unnecessary and unnecessary thoughts from your mind. Remove all thoughts that are irrelevant and unnecessary. Feel refreshed and fresh as you begin the process of clearing

and be full participation.

Telekinesis exercises you can test out

Many have fantasized about moving objects at will with just their minds (telekinesis). We have heard

The news is updated regularly. You can also discover videos posted on the web by people who claim to have

The ability to telekinesis was developed by the people who developed it. Yet, it doesn't seem to be to be real. Unfortunately, there are many of the

videos you see on the web are fake. Thanks to modern technology, it's simple to discover that a lot of

fake things. However, just because someone are able to fake certain things, does not necessarily mean that all telekinesis is

faked. Telekinesis is a skill which can be taught however, for the majority of people, it is

focused effort to achieve the first result. Because of this, the majority people quit after a while.

they see initial results.

However, by setting up a plan which begins by enhancing your focus first, and then gradually

Working on exercises that build the actual abilities of telekinetics and we're seeing significantly higher

Success rate.

Very few people have reached the level in their telekinesis instruction that they are able to reproduce regularly. However, thousands of people have been able to prove that

"something" that is not explained has occurred. The only rational explanation is that slowly , but surely,

People are developing their telekinesis skills.

The majority of people fail when they begin to make objects move, without any instruction.

immediately. The ones who have the most effective results from their telekinesis capabilities are those who have

extremely refined ability to concentrate. It is sensible to begin with fine-tuning your

ability to concentrate before you develop your telekinesis skills.

Concentration exercise: To do this exercise, you'll require a post-it-note. Put the post-it note down

A wall that is several feet from you, right at eye level. You can take a few seconds to allow your body and mind relax.

relax. Relax for a few minutes and then focus to the note. If you think of anything

When the thought comes to mind When they come to mind, gently move them away until only your image of the post-it note appears you.

your mind.

It might sound easy however, your objective is to get until you are able to keep the post-it

Note the image you have in your head without other thoughts intruding for at least five minutes.

Ideally, to keep it for 10 minutes, or longer.

It is interesting to know that those who regularly meditate are much more successful in

Concentrating and utilizing their telekinesis powers. It is because meditation is a way of concentration and accessing telekinesis abilities.

concentration and those who meditate often can remain focused for a long time.

more than 30 minutes or up to 30 minutes or. You will know when you've reached the point where you are concentrating completely with no distractions

Other thoughts or ideas that are circulating your mind over a prolonged period of time will then be prepared to

Begin to study how to telekinesis, and prepare to move the first object you encounter.

Groups can aid in developing your skills more quickly. There are numerous online communities,

But my students who are the best work as groups at their own local level. Invite a few of them.

Friends over to have friends over for a telekinesis celebration. Begin by building up concentration first. If you are having trouble,

If your group is brand new If you're a new group, it's best to dedicate a few hours only on concentration prior to

developing telekinesis capabilities. You'll see more effective results this way.

EXERCISE 1 The PSI-WHEEL

Paper2Required materials:

* A four-inch by four inch sheet of newspaper or Tinfoil.

• A pin, or a sewing needle.

* An eraser or cork.

The glass or jar or bowl.

Technique: Now poke the pin through the eraser to ensure that one side is facing upwards. Then fold the paper, or

Then, fold the tinfoil horizontally in half in a straight line, with the other side facing us. fold the top inwards and then fold it in half vertically. Then unfold. Once folded, fold

Again, but this time horizontally. Unfold and now our tinfoil or paper appears to be divided

into four parts. Turn the paper over and then fold it diagonally in half to form a triangle for the

The next step is to repeat the process for the opposite side. Then our tinfoil or paper appears to be divided into eight

parts. It'll look a bit of a shuriken or star.

Then we need to place the paper over the top of the pin , so that it spins. After that, we must remove the paper.

our minds and concentrate our concentration our attention on our eyes and focus on. It is important to alter our energy using our cells

It is in. It is our responsibility to allow it to become a part of us. When we believe that we are part of it and that it is us, we must attempt to

Move it as if you were moving an arm.

Note: Place a crystal transparent glass over the psi-wheel to ensure that neither air nor wind will be able to move the psi-wheel. Then

Imagine your hands or brain's energy flowing into the psi-wheel, which is at the cellular level. This makes it

Spin left or right.

EXERCISE 2 EXERCISE 2: PULLL/PEN

penRequired supplies:

* A pen

• A smooth surface on which to put the pen on

Method: Choose an item that is simple to move. Place it on the table. then sit straight and stand up straight, then make

Be careful not to hit the table. You can take a moment to calm your breathing and clear your mind. Make use of

the power of your mind to make the pen move over the desk. Find a variety of ways to connect with

The object: Imagine your brain's energy flowing in waves from your brain to your pen, and picture it.

The pen is rolling over the desk.

3. EXERCISE 3: THE CRORK

The materials required are:

* Cork or another substance that floats.

*A Bowl of water.

Method The method is identical to the exercises previously mentioned, but using different materials. Concentrate on

allowing the cork flow throughout the bowl.

It is important to note that this is not the same thing as Hydrokinesis. In Hydrokinesis you have to cause the water to move and also the

Cork is used to identify the direction of water's flow.

EXERCISE 4 PENDULUM

Materials required:

One String.

* One ring without stone or key.

Method: It's supposed to function as pendulums. It's the same as the other pendulums and we must try to

Move it forward and back, then move it with telekinesis.

Exercise 5 PAPER PUSH/PULL

Materials required:

* A piece of paper

* A surface to put the paper

Method:

Then fold the paper in half, then place it in a place where it can be seen.

Visualize the energy of strings joining and drawing all the power of paper. Visualize the paper either falling back toward you or moving away.

(Push) Pay attention to the paper that is pushing away from you like a magnet. think about the energy-string that is flowing through it.

forcibly pushing, and then with a sudden surge of force that resembles the explosive response.

(Pull) (Pull) sheet of paper that is falling, imagine that the string is sucking energy as an a

vacuum, but it is not only sucking, it moves close to your.

This method helps the brain learn the idea of pulling and pushing.

Exercise 6 FEATHER In A JAR

The materials required are:

* A feather

* A jar that has an lid

Method: To make this method you'll need a dry, clean container with lid and an unfurled feather. Put the feather inside the jar , and then place the lid on it so that you are sure there's no way that an unintentional gust of wind could infiltrate

The Jar. Place the container on the table the direction of your eyes and use the telekinesis device to move the feather or

float.

Keep in mind what we've talked about in earlier lessons as well as the exercises. Let your thoughts drift.

lower to the level of cellular and merge into the feather. Be aware of the strings inside

The feather. In your mind's eye let the power in your brain to raise only one of

The feather is lowered by strings at a given time until the whole feather is lifted, and it is able to

float.

If this doesn't work for you, think about visualizing your mind's energy as a breeze. Allow yourself to feel

the wind departs your body via the third eye of your body. The wind is blown through the jar, and then raise

The feather will rise into the air. Once you've got the feather up in the air, concentrate on using your brain to control the flight of the feather.

feather, which allows it to move up or down or side to side whenever you want, rather than floating around in the air.

it is begging to move.

7th EXERCISE: CANDLE FLAME BENDING

candles are required to be made of these materials:

* Candles

* Something to ignite the candle

Method: To perform this exercise you'll need candles and a lighter with and also an

The holder should be checked to ensure that it's stable and secure to the table front of your.

Set a candle on fire and place it on the table in front of you. It is best to place the flame just higher than the line of

vision, and is far enough from you so that your breath won't spark the flame.

Also, you should ensure that there aren't any drafts in the space. Switch off any fans that you are using in

The room should be closed and any windows that may be open. Let the candle be lit for a few minutes.

minutes to check whether there are any loose drafts.

The goal is to get the flame to bend. Bend the flame to only one side every time. You

Want to see a firm bent flame not just flickering to one side as if a wind was blowing.

across it.

Be sure to apply your mind's power to see your energy react with the flame of the candle.

cellular level. Once both energies are mingling and merged, let the power of your mind move the flame.

Exercise 8: CRUSHING A SODA CANN

Take an empty bottle of soda and place it down about two meters away. Keep your hand close to the can.

could be touched but not touching it.

Connect to the can, instead of a stream of energy create the whole hand.

The energy hand should be moved to the soda bottle and grasp it. Press the energy hand.

Spoon bending refers to the apparent deformation of objects, particularly cutlery made from metal, or with

physical force or lesser force than might normally be considered to be.

The bending of spoons attracted a lot of media attention in the 1970s as certain people claimed to have

the ability to trigger these incidents through paranormal psychic methods. Most notable was Uri Geller who had

The process involves bending metal spoons as well as keys made of steel as well as other items and substances.

Exercises in Hypnosis and Telepathy

How do you develop Telepathy

Telepathy is the capability to relay emotions, words or images to the mind of another. When

Although there isn't any evidence to suggest that telepathy is real, but you may still want to try it. Relax your mind and body,

Imagine that the recipient is directly in front of you and then focus your attention on sending them a message.

Words or images. Send and receive messages with a trusted person or a relative and keep track of

Keep track of your progress by keeping keep a record of your progress. After a few weeks of practice, you could be surprised to discover your partner and you

Have a strong connection to the mind. You've been told about people who are psychic. But what is it?

real? If so are you telepathic? What do you need to do to build your psychic exercises? Here are some suggestions for you.

steps to help you develop the ability to communicate.

Concentrating Your Thoughts

Relax your physical senses. You can try playing white noise using headphones, and wear blackout shades.

goggles. A shift in focus off of your bodily surroundings could allow you to concentrate on your vision

You should concentrate your attention focused on transmitting the telepathic message. Both you and the receiver must both work on tuning out your

senses. The loss of sensory stimulation can assist you in focusing your attention to the point.

Try stretching your muscles or doing yoga.

Sending the message via telepathic means requires the use of a lot of focus and concentration, so you should try to be physically and mentally

The mind is relaxed and the body is calm. Regular yoga and stretching will teach you how to relax and feel

A calm, focused state that is relaxed, focused and calm.

If you're preparing to transmit a message via telepathic communication Try stretching your arms, legs, and then back. Breathe deeply.

when you are in your pose, exhale slowly while pushing for 15 to 20 minutes. As you stretch,

Imagine all the tension that you have left your body.

Relax your mind by taking a moment to meditate. Wear loose-fitting clothing and sit in a comfortable posture.

Breathe slowly and exhale slowly, and try to rid your mind of thoughts that don't serve you. Try to imagine.

Scattered thoughts, random thoughts leave your head as you exhale.

Try to keep your attention on one idea. Try to meditate for at least 20 minutes every day.

After a few weeks of practice, it will become easier to concentrate your thoughts.

If you're in a calm focussed state, you're now ready to send an electronic message. Stay focused.

Keep in mind that both the sender and the receiver of the telepathic message must be relaxed and unblock their

minds.

Sending an Telepathic message

Visualize the person you want to send your message. Close your eyes and imagine the recipient as clearly as you can.

as possible. Make sure you imagine they as close to or sitting in your face. See details

using your eyes, like the eye color and the weight, height, and hair length and the way they

either stand or sit. If you're far from your receiver could be helpful to look up an image of them

Before you start visualizing them. When you create your mental picture and then forward your image to the recipient they

You should be able to relax and concentrate on listening for the messages. Request them to quiet their minds and imagine that you are there.

In front of them, with as much detail as they can.

Imagine how it feels to Talk to The Person.

Recall the emotions that you experience when you communicate with the person in person. Feel these feelings.

feelings as if the person felt as if they were in your presence. Be aware of these feelings and then believe in the

You are making a connection with another person.

Choose a simple idea or word. When you're beginning start with something easy for example, like an idea or word.

Nearby near the. Imagine it in as much detail as you can and then focus your attention only on it.

Focus on what it appears like, the way it feels to feel it touch and how you feel. [6]

Imagine an apple. Consider imagining an apple as clearly as you can through your eyes.

Imagine the taste and sensation of smacking the apple. Your attention should be solely focused upon the fruit.

Transmit your message.

Imagine the object moving from your mind to the receivers. Imagine yourself facing-to-face

With the receiver, tell them "Apple," or whichever idea you're sending. With the receiver, you can communicate

In your mind's eye, you can notice the expression of relief on their faces as they get what you're telling them.

them. Be aware of the distinction between straining and focusing. Focus on the

Mental image, but remain calm and relaxed. After you've thought it out let it go from your mind. Don't

Think about it again. Imagine giving it to the receiver and you're no longer holding it

onto it.

Request the recipient to write down the thoughts that come to their minds.

After you've sent your message, the recipient should remain open and relaxed until they realize that the message has been received.

The thought may have entered their thoughts. Then, they should record whatever thought thoughts have come to mind.

Before you check into the receiver, it is recommended to not forget to write down what you wanted to convey.

send. This can help you remain impartial when you compare your results.

Compare the results to each other. Once you're both prepared both of you must show each other the results.

and other things you've other than what you've. Don't be discouraged if you're not making it, particularly initially.

Spend some time clearing your mind. Then attempt to do it again using a different image.

Don't be down about yourself for not being able to convey a clear telepathic message. Try to be able to communicate clearly.

Have fun while you play!

The belief that telepathy is possible

At a minimum be sure to be open the possibility that a person may be telepathic.

skills. If you think it's not feasible your mind will work to ensure that you

Are you right? (unless your mind is truly evil, of course) you are right, and then it'll set out to

You are lying!)

Find a partner in practice

If you have a person close to you who would like to be telepathic, fantastic. If not, consider

You can search the internet for a forum for telepathy, and then join with someone on the forum. As with everything else, the more

You are able to practice, the better you improve your. A telepathy buddy can assist you in a variety of ways.

as well as the encouragement essential in the beginning stage.

Do it yourself

If you're unable to locate someone to talk with, don't be discouraged. There are many ways that you can try the art of telepathy.

by yourself. For example, you could make a shuffle of a deck of cards, then lay them out face-down and then play

Your newfound abilities to identify your new-found abilities to identify which card is it. Telepathy cards are easily available.

Downloads you can get access to that will enhance your telepathy abilities on your own.

Little practice, and frequently

As you begin, it puts an enormous strain on your brain So, keep your practice sessions brief. Additionally, you should make

Make sure that you have a good energy level prior to starting - some exercises can help.

Take a look at ESP test cards.

You can purchase them on the internet, and even Amazon sells them so don't fret over finding ESP cards.

Use these as a practice to build confidence.

Relax and unwind.

Sometimes , when we're learning about something we've never done before, we may try too difficult. You've probably been there before. The

The harder you attempt harder, the more difficult the task becomes, and your frustration will are. Relax. Let it

Accept that you're not as great as you'd like and especially

If you're just beginning to develop when you're just beginning to learn about telepathy. If you're looking for more advice on letting go and relax you, read this article

Use the Sedona technique and you'll feel chilled in no time.

You can use telepathy in your dreams

This is because you're not restricted to using telepathy only in the state of consciousness. You can master the art of controlling

Begin by keeping a dream diary in which you list your ideas the moment you get up

up. The more you practice this and the more your goals will be recognized. You will then begin to be rewarded

Telepathic dreams in your dreams They can come from all kinds of places However, there are many who

Reports of receiving them from family members and friends who have passed "to an alternate side".

Training with Your Partner

Have a go at trying to send or receive texts. Alternate your roles as you go through the process and test if you can master it.

You are more successful in either. You might find that you're better at gaining

messages that your friend is more adept in messaging, and your friend is better at. It's beneficial to practice

Someone you trust, for example an intimate friend or a relative.

Play a Card Game.

Pick five cards that are unique for example, playing cards or cards that have images on them. You and your companion will be in a

Separately, choose one of the cards randomly. Calm your mind and relax in a separate location, and then focus your attention exclusively

by sending the card's picture for your friend to send the image.

Your partner should be able to calm their thoughts and be able to sense the message. If they sense that an idea has been conceived, they should

In their minds, ask them to take note of the card you gave them to them, and then look up your results.

Draw an Image, then Send it to your partner.

Create a sketch of a shape, or a simple combination of conditions such as a circle inside the triangle. Make sure you are focusing

your thoughts about the body, and imagine the image moving through your mind towards your companion's. If you are

They feel they've been notified, ask them to draw whatever image they've thought of.

Alternately, another person could create an image and then show it to the sender who then tries to send this information to the recipient.

You should keep A Telepathy Journal To Track Your Progression.

When you try to talk to someone telepathically, note down the specifics of your communication. Notify who

the sender and receiver and what the image you received was and whether you were

successful. A journal can assist you in improving your skills.

Even if the attempt was unsuccessful, take note of any details that seem promising. For example, if the message was

"apple" Your friend wrote "red" and "fruit," that's a excellent indication!

Hy NoSIS Exercises

Eye Cues

There are two parts of the brain. The left one is responsible for those with a more "creative" side, and the left manages the more "conscious" part the left manages the more "creative" and conscious side, and

The left is the "practical" and unconscious. In every conversation, we are looking for feedback from

listener to observe how they react to our comments. Pay attention to the eyes of the listener. Are they looking at the

right, which is accessing the conscious, or for the subconscious? Are they focused on a specific thing in

The room? If they're accessing their unconscious, you could claim that they aren't aware of their surroundings.

We are aware of.

Visualization

The visualization of rooms can be used for trance-inducing purposes and also to suggest ideas. For instance, you can you can ask your

The subject is to think of a room they are familiar with. Imagine every single detail of the room including the floor,

The windows' shape and the design of your wall, and the scent and the lighting. After that, you can move to a room

They're less experienced with. When they are unable to remember the precise details, they allow the mind to

suggestion.

Advanced Tips:

* Recall positive memories using visualization. positive memories.

They are often associated with reward behavior.

Change the perception one has of an image that is negative.

Eye Fixation

Have you ever been "zoning off" and focusing on something interesting in the room?

Are you listening to someone's conversation? Have you missed the words they're using? You could have been in a state of trance. Anything could have happened.

An object in focus can be used to create the state of trance. One of the most well-known examples is"power pendulum" or "power pendulum" or

A "swinging pocket watch" -- though these two items are connected with hokey stage

hypnosis. You are more likely to fall short and experience resistance with these types of objects because of their

reputation.

However, there are two main reasons why eyes are fixed. First, the object is able to keep the mind in a state of consciousness.

The mind is occupied, opening to the possibility of. The eyes also become physically exhausted when

They fixate or move around. For example: Try looking upwards at the ceiling for several minutes

(without bend the neck). The eyes naturally wear out and close.

Breathing Countdown

You might have heard about breathing exercises that are controlled for meditation, but it's be an effective method of

self-hypnosis.

Here's how it will work:

* Close your eyes , and sit up straight in your chair with your arms in your lap.

* Breathe deeply through the nose and then exhale by the mouth.

* By breathing slowly and controlled count down from 100.

Each exhale counts as one time.

Then, at the end of the day you could be in a state of trance. If not, you can continue the process of in a downward direction from a higher

number.

Chapter 7: Hypnotic Induction Techniques

1. Magnetic Hands

1. Begin by using your hands to generate warmth.

2. Once you notice the heat, you can pull you hands away until you are about 4 inches away from each other.

3. Then, move your hands gently between them, until you feel the magnetic pull that comes from nature. It will

It feels like you are a feel like a magnet. Pay attention to those sensations until they become stronger and more powerful.

4. Explore this energy until can feel that your hands desire to connect. This is the moment to

Close your eyes and then deepen your sleep from there.

5. It doesn't matter if you hands meet or are 10 inches apart. What you're searching for

Here is a powerful magnetic attraction. If your hands don't touch then focus on that space.

Enhance the enhance the.

Exploring energy in a way such as this is a great method of keeping the mind occupied

to allow your subconscious to take over, allowing you to unwind and fall into an euphoric Trance.

The Power Pendulum

Pendulums are a potent method of communicating with the subconscious mind and induce the state of trance. You can

Buy a basic pendulum from any store that sells new age products or make your own. If you own already a pendant

It is easy to change it into a powerful pendant. Any chain that is adorned with stones or other object that is hanging

It can also be used to create an oscillator. You can also make use of the string by tying it onto the bolt or nut

From your toolbox.

1. Start by finding a suitable position. Keep the pendulum in between your index finger and thumb,

keeping it in place with no chain or thread from your fingers.

2. Make sure your elbow is floating freely and is not sitting on the table, or locked in position. Relax your shoulders.

And loose, and then begin getting comfortable with the movement that your pendulum has.

3. The instructor "will" allow the pendulum be moved by keeping your attention on the movement in both directions. You can

You can tell your pendulum that it should start moving, and it will.

4. Be sure to keep your mind free. Do not try to hard, as your mind can get stuck.

The method.

5. Approach this with a relaxed and easy way.

6. When it begins to move then put your eyes shut and let the pendulum drop to the floor, and after that

Begin your practice the way you would normally do; for instance, start with affirmations or visualizations.

Pantomimed Mentalization

This is a variation on the two previous exercises, but this time, you'll be adding an additional dimension to your

mentalization: you'll use pantomime to describe the space. For instance, when you imagine the

room, you might tell yourself:

"The space is huge (spread your arms to make this clear) and there's an entrance through it.

The left. To my right is the window. I'm going to open it." (Go by the motions of

Opening to the windows.)

The idea is to enhance your mind by using physical and speech.

After a few repetitions you'll learn to make your perception of the unfamiliar as authentic as it can be.

You're already familiar with them. Keep in mind that the more mental abilities you develop the sharper your

Awareness will grow.

The most common mistakes to avoid when studying Telekinesis

The biggest mistake nearly everyone makes with Telekinesis The two most common traps that can befall people.

If you want to learn telekinesis, there are a few traps to into. If you make one of these mistakes I'll guarantee you that

You'll never grow your mind to reach the level that you're capable. You'll

You can still utilize your telekinetic abilities in a certain degree, however not to the degree it's

possible. This is why we have two most frequently made errors that are made.

Let other people convince you that the concept of telekinesis isn't an actual fact.

If you allow others to say that you shouldn't accomplish it, or that it's impossible...guess that you've let them know you've provided them with a false impression.

control over your thoughts and beliefs and can inform you what's feasible to you.

You and what they're trying to tell you is the best feasible and isn't possible for them. Suggestions

from other people can be contagious--
especially negative, limiting, or hurtful ideas
and beliefs.

Don't ever give your power away as that.

Don't let them be too limiting and let them
believe what they want to believe. If you start
to believe in their beliefs,

Then you'll be able to see the limitations of
their abilities. If they're not sure what to do
does not mean they aren't capable.

it's impossible. At one time, everybody believed
the world was flat as well. Then we've all come
around.

Be aware that this isn't completely the case.

It's possible to get people saying, "That's a
trick" or "Well If it's true, then take this chair."

It's not your responsibility to engage them or
convince them they're right If they believe it's
great...and it is if

Not necessarily, but that's their decision. Your
beliefs will become the truth for you. If you
listen to what others say.

You decide what you do, you're letting them determine your existence and the way you live. As you'll

You will begin to notice more clearly... I'm convinced that money comes effortlessly to you. You'll soon begin to move it

toward you... I'm sure people will like you, and they'll draw them towards you as well.

If you think that people do not like you or it's difficult to make...you put it off just

just as you draw it.

It's important to know that you're able to move objects with your Mind. If you're struggling with trouble with your mind,

If you are having a difficult time dealing with beliefs that limit you within your own life, you may be interested in looking into the resources available at

My site. Destroy your limitations here.

Expecting HUGE results too quickly.

You may have watched a movie in which people drive a car using their minds for instance, Star Wars and the force, and you considered, "Wow I want to be able to accomplish this." Many people are caught up in the trap of

Wanting to complete these kinds of things immediately and get frustrated when they're unable to accomplish it.

after just 10 minutes of practice after which you begin to think it's not feasible. The same thing happens in movies.

but that's not to say it's impossible, but it's possible...that sort of thing,

however, will require longer to develop and practice your abilities. If you expect to see huge results, it will take time.

From the beginning, they often give up and then think, "This doesn't work."

(A Limiting assumption) This is then applicable to those who have it. They'd like to run before they've realized they can.

to slow. It's a guarantee that when you've got that mental image in your mind... your body will begin

right...and it won't work for you. Telekinesis just like everything else is a process of learning. You

You had need to walk before you were able to climb and you fell down lots of times before you was able to walk. I

There isn't a person alive who can walk for 20 minutes.

Be aware that what you're about to be doing at the very first step towards learning and

developing your skills. It's the smallest part that you can build. It's the very first building block.

From that block then you can place another block and begin to build upon the foundation that you've created. After you

If you were a newborn likely took several months before you could get ability to balance and walk a few steps.

feet and not fall down. It is important to remember that everyone must begin somewhere. I would also like you to realize this

By using the analogy of the weight training... If a person starts exercising with weights, they do not enter into

go to the gym on the first day, and you can bench press the entire stack of weights.

(And If they do to do so, there's a high possibility of serious injuries occuring.) This is also true for

building your mental capacity. It is essential to practice and improve your ability to think. When you're capable

for moving a tiny object before when you finish this article however, this doesn't mean that you'll have to

be capable of moving a car in that same day. If you'd like to truly improve your skills and abilities,

You must practice it.

Once you've honed your ability, once you witness it taking place... You'll take ownership of it, and it's right there with you.

to live your life to enjoy it at any time you wish to. Similar to riding a bike Once you've got the

talent... it's a skill that you'll possess the ability to master it.

Self-reflection

Doing things yourself. This is a part of the education for telekinesis. It is particularly among beginners. There isn't a reliable formula to explain the mechanism of telekinesis This is

that many are left to discover and explore their individual characteristics. Study on

Telekinesis is crucial in guiding you in the right direction about the process itself but you also require

self-reflection that actually helps you overcome.

What that means is that you'll know everything you need to know about the telekinesis process, but you will not know the rest

regarding the likelihood that it will go according to plan is dependent on your own. That's why you require moments of

self-reflection will assist you better understand yourself. You'll be able to make a decision on

What you're thinking about and understand the reasons behind what you're thinking about and understand the reasons behind. The results will reveal more

significantly increasing your odds in achieving success with telekinesis. This is because having a good understanding of

Your self-worth is more often accompanied by self-esteem, which is crucial in the world generally and

as well as being successful at the art of telekinesis.

Doing this step, then is a blunder to avoid when you make the decision to give it a go

telekinesis. Many people are more at achieving the point at which they can move

Things, however, the best things take time to complete and require taking the appropriate steps.

While this appeal may seem natural and strong, you must be determined to follow the right procedure

Increase your chances of your goals.

Proper focus

It is essential to focus properly to be able to develop Telekinesis, even though it is essential in a variety of

different areas of your areas of your. People tend to concentrate on putting into lots of effort. They are not aware of their

When people think about something, they usually try to incorporate muscle power into the process. This is particularly the case

Telekinesis is a case in point since the functions that are expected to be completed need force even in normal

Situations, however, the rules are changed, which is why mental analysis is essential in this case. If circumstances don't work out as expected,

Human nature is to push harder and it is not difficult to set up an endless cycle that leads to

which can cause tension and anger to a lot of stress and frustration, which isn't helping by doing telekinesis.

The best method to gain concentration is to remain in a state of relaxation. Sit somewhere, unwind and let your mind open

your mind. It will create of space in your mind and you will be able to have space to breathe.

This is the best moment to take your object and attempting to move or manipulate it in the manner you would like.

Do not think about it too much Instead, simply feel the

experience. The next step is that you'll begin to feel the object, and you will feel as if you are experiencing an

connection to the internet. It's not even necessary to try to find out the nature of this connection since you have no

could divert your attention on the problem.

If you've got this connection Try to make the object move. It is possible to imagine that the force on the

object that is gently touching it or it could be an inborn energy that is starting to flow. Try to create this

imagination as realistic as is possible. This is a crucial factor because it's the

the point at which most people doubt the legitimacy of what they are doing or attempt to justify it,

This could cause problems for the whole process.

Don't get too harsh on yourself as you'll be required to work on this for a while before you can be confident.

get better at getting better at it. If you have practiced this you will be more likely to move.

However, do not hang the hope too long, as you could end up disappointed because

The results cannot be guaranteed and at other times, it might require time.

Common Mistakes in Communication

These mistakes are common and can lead to the communication to break down. You don't

Know the reason. There are a lot of errors made...way way too numerous to mention here But here are three of them.

The most popular ones.

You think that the other person is understanding precisely what you're trying to convey.

This is a big one... Communication is the only way to make people move in the direction you want them to go.

What you want them to do is to be in the same space with you. What I mean by that is you're communicating with them in a manner that

they can understand the meaning of what they are hearing. Be aware of this when communicating it is important to master this skill, you must learn it.

ability, you assume responsibility for the sending as well as the acceptance in the transmission.

Have you ever been in an argument that was heated with another person only to realize you had been talking about exactly the same thing?

Similar to the same thing, but in a different manner? It's absurd, but yet it is happening often. It sounds absurd, but it is true.

The other person thought they thought they understood you point...and but the truth is they were not sure what you meant.

There was something else that the incident.

Chapter 8: Mastering Telekinesis

Based on my own experiences, telekinesis is real. But for me, it's been hit-and- missed throughout the many years. I've learned some important lessons however. For instance, I've observed other teachers teaching telekinesis, and many think it's the sole focus of only one purpose of mentally pushing , spinning an object. For me, however the intense concentration just consumed my mental energy. It's much more easily when you don't have to think about it.

Naturally, I place myself in what I consider to be "The zone" before I attempt the move of an object. However, once I'm within the zone I just consider what I would like to achieve, and visualize it happening in my head as if I could go forward by a couple of seconds or minutes, and finish the task. After I've gotten the mental image of the task completed I then return to my present state of time and space , and in my mind "ask" that object I want to work with to move the way I've instructed. In the end, the concept of telekinesis is a connection between the person who is telekinetic (you) as well as the thing you want to move. After I've requested this and the object moves, it will move to my liking.

That's the strategy we'll be using to create a symbiotic connection between your telekinetic self and the object or relationship if you like, as described by the character of John Travolta George Malley, in the film, Phenomenon. I've always thought that his explanation of why the sunglasses spin and float was artistic and precise.

Another thing I learned was that heat could be part in the movement of an object. For instance, consider for instance the Egely Wheel, which is an amazing tool for developing your telekinetic capabilities which we'll employ in the exercises of this book. It's easy to allow this wheel to spin without touching it as long as your hand is near to the edge.

This is done by changing our mental state to make our subconscious and conscious mind are in as to be "in-tune" in tune with universal consciousness and thus "in that zone." Some describe this state as an hypnagogic state. I don't believe that I'm"hypnotized" when I've changed my mental state to become energy-wise "in tuned" in tune with my universal mind. I'm just in tune and ready to perform at a high level of conscious performance in my kinetic events.

To get into the zone, it's extremely easy if you take these easy steps:

1. Find your comfortable zone by first wearing loose clothes, like pajamas, then selecting the location where you want to rest your body and prepare for your astral journey (your mattress, a comfy chair and so on.) You should ensure that there aren't any distracting factors like light sources or the sound of a TV.

2. Close your eyes, and then begin to pant. We will pant until we reach 100. Each count will be comprised of two inhales and one exhale. In other words, you will keep count from 1-100 as, "1(inhale-exhale), 2(inhale-exhale), 3(inhale-exhale)....100(inhale-exhale).

3. When you sweat, picture three small white balls of light. One is below the belly button One in the center the chest area, as well as the third directly behind your eye. Imagine each one growing larger as you pant, and expanding upwards, downwards, forwards, and backwards. At the age of 20 imagine these spheres interspersed and merging at the time of 40, the three have grown so big that they've morphed into one ball of light that covers your body in a blanket of light that is so bright it's overwhelming.

4. Next, think of the image of a white hot bolt of lightning that reaches at the very top of your head. It's from the universe that is spreading across every meridian and vein. You've seen lightning flash across the sky and spread out. Imagine that similar branching out inside your body. The radiant white heat will not cause harm or burn; it cleanses and energizes your body. You can feel and see it cleansing every cell in your body. This lightning bolt and glowing sphere are purifying your energy and physical bodies, flushing out the meridians and chakras, as well as reconnecting you with the source. When you reach 60 the all-encompassing lightning bolt cleansed the entire body.

5. When you continue to sweat you will be able to see another version of yourself inside your body, an energy copy as a tiny babythat is cradled inside your stomach. The astral body is what you are. Let it expand and be fed by the white sphere and lightning until it has grown completely and you feel it pressing on your skin. Allow it to penetrate into the skin's pores to extend beyond your body into your white light sphere. You can feel this slightly larger body moving up to three inches of your skin, and creating the physical body inside the light sphere. The expansion will be evident at the age of 80.

6. After you have worked towards 100, look for the silver cord in you that connects your astral self and your bodily body. What is it that you can see? Are you able to connect your two bodies to your crown? Your heart? In your Solar Plexus? I'm not going to inform you "where it connects" Since I would like you to determine on your own. Naturally, with the two bodies so close the cord is very thin however, it is able to extend anywhere in the universe you want to go, keeping both bodies connected. When you are at 100, exhale an exhale that is large and feel the warmth and energy that is flowing through you. Be aware that you don't have to be at a specific point in the 20th or 40th, 60th or even the 80th pant. It's just important that you complete the entire process. This means that if you want to go beyond 100, it is okay. However, at least 100 is the standard.

7. We will now learn to change our mental state to bring our subconscious and conscious mind in tune with the universal consciousness, in order to enter the zone and be aligned to the source for all information and energy. Keep a pencil straight to your face, about three to four inches away of distance from the eyes. It is also necessary to have an additional focal point that is that is at least 10 feet away. It could be a TV screen, a candle lit or even an alarm clock, so

long as it's within your view. The first step is to focus on the pencil , until it is in focus. After that, turn your attention away from the pencil and throw your eyes out of the focus of the pencil. You will then focus on the TV screen, candle or the alarm clock. Then, shift your attention once more on the pencil. Slowly return your attention to the television, candle or even the alarm clock but remain at the center of your attention! Your vision will shift to another in the world and your concentration will shift to a distance between your pencil and the television. It's as if you has expanded to encompass both focal points simultaneously. The pencil appears like you're looking through a magnifying glass as your secondary focus shifts from blurry to focus. If this happens, then you've been in the area.

Please note that you may notice two fingers instead one or two TV displays, candles or or alarm clocks, or candles as you shift your attention from one spot to another. That's normal. However when you are in synch, you'll only see one when you've locked between these two points and have entered the zone. It is my belief that this practice alters the brain's waves and assists our minds understand the relationship between all things. I don't have any proof of this however, my gut has convinced me that it is the case.

If I perform the steps mentioned above and feel a sense of calm and a connection to all of the universe. I have used the same seven steps I've used in other books to increase the accuracy of pendulums and connecting to the healing energy of other people, which is why you'll read this chapter on my various blueprints.

When you're prepared to start developing your kinetic skills You'll find 21 exercises on the next pages that will help you improve your skills from the simplest of tasks, and even beyond. Although this book is mostly focused on developing telekinesisskills, you'll also find exercises to develop other kinetic skills, including electrokinesis, aerokinesis and pyrokinesis. I believe they're all interconnected in the way we affect or alter energy fields that surround us. I believe that energy fields and a variety of skills related to kinetics will cross paths once your body and mind have connected and worked together to strengthen the connection between them.

Make sure you spend at least three days doing each exercise. Some may consider three days of exercise to be is a lot, particularly in the case that you've learned an exercise on the first day. I can assure you that it's not. Also, don't be surprised if certain exercises require your time to understand. The quickest method to improve your skills is this:

1. Spend 33 minutes a day to complete each exercise for three consecutive days and learn how to perform the exercise in the order in which they are given.

2. Set an alarm for 33 minutes for your training session. In this period, you must have absolute silence! I would suggest shutting off your television, switching off your music, as well as closing your cell phone to remain in a space that is completely quiet in which your mind can become more settled and focus on the job to be completed.

3. After three days, move onto the next exercise. Even if it is the case that you did not succeed with any particular exercise, you can continue to do it again after three days.

4. This is where it can become intense. You must devote at least 3 minutes for each previous exercise, and practiced in order prior to starting the 33 minutes of training time for your current exercise. That means that if you're in the 11th exercise you'll have 10 exercises

which will be practiced for 3 minutes prior to starting your 33-minute workout for exercise 11. In the event that you've got an alarm installed on your smartphone, you can set it to sound at three minutes intervals and the final exercise being set at 33 minutes.

5. If you fail to succeed in completing an exercise within the time frame of 3 days Do not be discouraged. You're still learning even if it seems to be failure. You'll be successful with one of your three-minute sessions.

6. While you are working on each exercise, stay present and connected to the activity. Don't attempt to force a result You can ask the object to cooperate with youand "allow" that desired outcomes to occur. After that, visualize it happening in your head. This is a link between energy sources that are connected. We are not the sole master over the ability to telekinetically move as we are partners to make a shift in energy force regardless of whether it's the partnership of an unrolled pencil across the table, an erupting flame or a telekinetic feather. Remember this when you move forward.

7. Be aware that you must take the time to complete the exercise even if it seems too long. Once you've completed Exercise 21, you'll be

spending 93 minutes enhancing your abilities but you'll be able to complete it. After you've spent 3 days of Exercise #21 it will be reduced to 63 minutes the time you'll need to practice until you've learned the 21 exercises.

Before we begin you must read the instructions for each exercise thoroughly. There are a few things that you will require, including magnets, aluminum foil, as well as An Egely Wheel. Once you've got the items you'll be prepared. Keep in mind that there is only one new exercise for each 3-day period, for 63 consecutive days in one row. This may seem like an old story however it's important...Each new exercise will last for 33 minutes, whereas any prior exercise is only three minutes. For instance, on Day 7 of the week, you'll start your exercise routine by completing Exercise #1, then three minutes for Exercise #2, then ending with 33 minutes of Exercise #3.

Always begin your day with exercise #1 and work toward the new workout. It is easy to calculate the time that your alarm will ring at the right time. For instance, on days 7 and 9, if you choose to start your exercise at 10AM, you could schedule your alarm for 10:03, 10:06 10, 10:03 or 10:06 and 10:39. Let's begin.

Days 1-3/Exercise 1: Connecting to Your Energy Field

This first activity might be familiar to those who have been reading my book The Energy Healing Blueprint. If you're already a proficient healer, you're aware of the feeling of healing energy around your hands and body and you already know how you can "feel" your energy field. No matter if you're familiar with it or not these next 3 days are all about connecting with our own energy field. Let's start our day with a workout:

1. For the first time begin by rubbing your palms together for ten to fifteen seconds in order to warm your palms.

2. Then, you should pull your hands apart slightly from each other (roughly six to 12 inches) as you imagine your hands are an magnet to the opposing force. As you move your hands to each other, imagine that you be able to feel your hands feel the "push" between them, trying to push the hands to separate. When you tear them apart you will notice you can feel that "push" disappears with increasing distance, and becomes stronger when you return them to each other.

The process is easy. While your fingers move from one place to the next you're creating energy, particularly when you imagine the ebb and flow the pull and push the energy is creating when you put your hands together and then separate them.

When you let this energy grow, you will begin to feel the energy manifesting beyond the vision that the force of magnetism. There will be a warm and tingling sensation in your hands, indicating the energy that is flowing between them.

If you're struggling to feel this sensation, you could utilize purchase discs or bar magnets to perform the exercise. Keep them in your hands, with identical polarities facing one opposite for"pushing," and "pushing" sensation with opposite polarities facing one another to experience"pulling" or "pulling" experience. When your hands and mind are accustomed to the physical sensations that the magnets provide, you can put them away and then return your attention to the energy that is flowing between your hands.

Actually, you should stop now and buy some magnets because they'll prove very useful for this exercise. Do not worry if you've already completed this exercise. You are able to finish the exercise, buy magnets and utilize them later during the three minutes of your sessions. However, for those with a few smaller magnets, you can place one in each hand, and then bring them closer to each other. Will they "push" in a push or "pull" off of one others?

If the identical magnetic polarities are facing each other, they'll pull away. If the opposite polarities are facing each one another and they are attracted, they will and pull each other. Try both opposite polarities. When they pull away move them closer so that you can feel the powerful pushing sensation. If they pull toward one another, hold onto your magnets and bring them close as you can without touching.

After you've spent a while playing with the magnets, set them back down and recall every sensation. Then, try to feel the same sensations with your hands without gloves by imagine that your palms have similar opposite polarities (pushing) before you having opposite Polarities (pulling).

The mind is able to alter the direction of the flow of energy through each hand. This is extremely beneficial to healing and energy work. That is the reason this particular book is also able to work together along with The Energy Healing Blueprint.

After you've spent 33 minutes developing this strong energy connection between your hands and your hands, you can spend your day with your hands and feel the energy of different objects. It could be your beloved cat, flowers in vase, or an unfinished pencil sitting on a table. Just run your fingers around the area of the object without touching the object.

Don't be shocked if you notice, for instance, that when you're feeling the force of a pencil, it strays away from your palm. Telekinetic abilities is often swiftly observed in situations where you don't try to influence the outcome, but instead being aware of the direction you want the object to go (to you away from you or turning).

In this moment, an alternative, though the most recommended could be to "see" the energy of your hands. The energy field that surrounds every object is called the aura. It is important to note that attempting to perceive the aura is only a suggestion step since it will be discussed within my books including The Extra Sensory Perception Blueprint. Your 33-minute exercise includes steps 1 and 2 without and with magnets. Visually detecting auras is a very important option that is highly recommended.

End your day by reflecting over your 33 minutes. The outcome, whether you achieved it or not is not important. The process of developing telekinesis and connecting to energy fields requires time, so be aware that regardless of the results of your practice and your skills in the exercise will increase each day!

Day 4-6/Exercise #2"Creating Energy Spheres

I've heard many Telekinesis practitioners talk about creating energy spheres. They are also known as Psi balls. They are energy balls, like that of the Orb of Life that my personal healer, Shiva Love, creates for his clients. In this session we'll do something similar to making the Orb of Life, albeit slightly different. In this exercise, we'll extend Exercise 1 by expanding the energy field in our hands , resulting in three dimensions of energy-spheres.

Three energy spheres constitute three energy spheres that comprise our "core" energy sphere which ranges between an average size softball up to an entire volleyball as well as an "micro" energy sphere that is similar to golf balls down to a marble and an "personal fields" energy sphere that is so big that it encompasses your entire body, stretching over you in perfect size, with a slight dip towards the Earth and slightly higher than your head, then out towards our sides to be the same height as our energy-sphere.

Be aware that before beginning the exercise today, you must spend three minutes practising the exercises you did on Days 3 and 4. Today, you may prefer setting your alarm for 33 minutes, in 11 minute intervals, as we will be performing three exercises in one. Let's begin:

Energy Sphere 1. Core Energy SphereFirst, let's begin with a standard-sized energy sphere. It is the center of your energy or your "core" in your energy center. It is the way it is developed:

1. Make sure to rub your hands in a circular motion to increase the amount of energy flowing through your palms. Note: From this exercise onward, you must always use your hands to stimulate your energy prior to beginning any telekinesis exercise.

2. Spread your hands about 4-8 inches apart. Imagine the energy flowing in your palms. Feel it grow in brightness and warmth between your palms and forming into an elongated globe.

3. As the energy accumulates and expands, imagine an emitted light ball moving in your hands. As you're working in a quiet space be sure to listen for the humming sound that the resonance (also known as the sound or frequency) that it creates when you construct it. Every thing produces sound, like a flute played to a stone lying in the soil; you must just listen.

4. Let this piece of energetic energy grow into the perfect energy sphere in accordance with your soul. Check to see if it's developing into the size of a softball, or growing bigger. The size generally falls between the size of a softball to the basketball or volleyball.

5. If you believe that the energy growing to its maximum capacity and you feel it is no longer needed, remove it from your body as you think of a person or loved one who might need an energy boost to heal an illness, to improve their mood or get them over a roadblock in life. That is, give the energy field towards the person that is in your mind, as they are in need of it. This is a method to increase your own energy and increase your capacity to attract more.

6. Only 11 minutes will be spent on creating your energy sphere's core before moving on to that micro-energy-sphere.

The Energy Sphere 2. Micro Energy Sphere- It is now time to construct the condensed version of your primary energy sphere. It's similar to the process described above. The procedure is like this:

1. Repeat the rub to release the energy into your palms.

2. Spread your hands about 4-8 inches apart. consider the energy that is accumulating in your palms. Feel it expanding in brightness and warmth between your palms. It will then gather into an oblong.

7. As the energy accumulates and forms, picture an energy ball that is pulsating between your fingers.

8. Let this piece of energetic energy grow into the perfect energy sphere in accordance with your own inner self.

9. When you are satisfied that it at its maximum "core" capacity then don't let it go out. Keep this energy core within your grasp, in the same way you envision it shrinking into the smallest

sphere of energy condensed and light, about the dimensions of golf balls, or smaller.

10. Once it's compressed Look around your space and the condensed sphere of energy exploding into an object that is easily moved. Perhaps you've set an unfinished pencil on a table. Then, send it flying at the pencil like you were throwing marble or a golf ball into the pencil. Visualize in your mind the condensed energy ball hitting the pencil, causes it to move.

11. Only 11 minutes are needed to the creation of your micro-energy field before getting to your personal energy sphere.

Energy Sphere #3 3: The Personal Field Energy Sphere- For the final 11 minutes of your set, we will discover how to increase your energy field to create your own "personal energy field" to help energize and safeguard your. Follow these steps:

1. Re-rub your hands to release the energy into your palms.

2. Spread your hands apart 4-8 inches and consider the energy that is accumulating within your fingers. Feel it grow in brightness and warmth between your palms. It will then gather into the shape of a circle.

3. As the energy accumulates and forms, picture the light ball pulsing in your hands.

4. Allow this piece of energetic energy grow into the perfect energy sphere according to your soul.

5. When you are satisfied that it at its maximum "core" capacity then don't let it go out. Keep the energy source in your hands in the way that you imagine it shrinking into tiny spheres of energy condensed and light, about the dimensions of golf balls, or smaller.

6. When it's compact, don't throw the energy sphere you have condensed at anything. Instead, hold the sphere with your hands and then push the energy sphere in your body towards your sternum. Feel the warm feeling of energy in the core in your physique. Within you, let it to expand to its original dimensions that was Energy Sphere #1, or your energy sphere that is your core. Feel your core vibrating and nourishing the body's energy.

7. When it is back to its "core" size It is then allowed to continue growing. You will see the energy sphere expanding until it fills your entire body . It then becomes so big that it seeps into your body, making it glowand continues to grow until it is no longer at the center of your

body it is now at it's center in a perfect circle filled with energy, which feeds and shields you.

8. The energy is charging each part of your body, both inside and outside. When you're completely encased in the energy sphere stay focused on the sensations of being charged and connected to the energy ball until your 33 minute alarm sounds. That's right, you'll spend the remaining 11 minutes soaking in your cocoon of safety.

When you're done with the first day of the second workout, think about your accomplishments. Do you have a vague idea of it ?...OR...Are you beginning to sense the connection? No matter what I would like to congratulate you for working towards a remarkable objective; and you have two days left to make energy spheres over the course of 33 minutes. :)

Days 7 to 9/Exercise 3: Working on Energy Wheels

Today , we are learning how to move objects by using the energy field. The easiest method to start getting results is using what's called an energy wheel also known as the Psi wheel.

Before beginning today's exercise be aware that you have six minutes of exercise to complete prior to starting Exercise #3. There is a three-minute block for Exercise 1 and a three-minute block in Exercise 2. It's the final time I'll practice this. The new exercise should not begin until you've practiced for 3 minutes each exercise previously completed. Let's get moving.

If you are you are practicing for 33 minutes, you may switch from one to the other your PSI wheel as well as your Egely wheel. If one wheel is more efficient than the other one, you should focus on the one that's more difficult. Even if you already own the Egely wheel or standard Psi wheel, I would like you to create your own. There's an element of fun for making your own energy wheel. It is believed to create a link between our telekinetic subconscious desire and our energy wheel. Each day, think about your achievements.

Days 10-12/Exercise 4 Suspended Psi Wheel

In this experiment we will be working to move a suspended object with force. This is why we'll first construct a larger Psi wheel.

1. Make a thin sheet of cardboard, such as the kind used in packaging for T-shirts. Cut two 1-1/2-inch lengthwise strips across the cardboard.

2. Join them in a cross-shaped pattern at the center. Once the glue is dry then bend the four arms to the downwards at a 45-degree angle.

3. Our aim is to place the Psi wheel at chest-high So, find a spot in your home that you can hang an extension string from the ceiling all the way to the massive Psi wheel. Once you've found the spot take a measurement of how long of string needed and in excess to tie to the ceiling.

4. Make a hole at the center the Psi wheel, and put one end across the upper. Pull one foot of extra through the hole. This will give you enough room to tie a knot at the very end to stop the string from sliding back down the massive Psi wheel.

5. The next step is to then hang then your Psi wheel and place yourself before it. Rub your hands together to increase the power, then slowly lift them onto that of the Psi wheel. Similar to exercise 3 try to make the Psi wheel turn in every direction.

6. When you are able to spin the wheel, move your fingers between the Psi wheel so that it can spin back and forth, like the pendulum that swings YES or NO. Actually, you've created a massive Psi wheel pendulum, however it is not

our intention to inquire about it and instead to focus on the motion. But, for those who have read the book I wrote, The Pendulum Dowsing Blueprint You can keep this massive Psi wheel in place and utilize it in the future to serve as an "house pendulum",

7. Take your time and be in complete focus, frequently changing hands while you work on shifting your massive Psi wheel around.

After three days of training I am certain that you'll get that big Psi wheel moving. If you don't like always don't worry just move to the next workout after your three-day practice. With time, you'll be able to master these kinetic exercises since you're gaining capabilities with each day of training.

Days 13-15/Exercise 5- Pushing/Pulling Aluminum Foil

Conclusion

Many people have different opinions they have to share about the phenomenon of telekinesis regards to its real or not.

There are those who are able to confirm the reality that it does exist, and they've either

Have you been able to do this or have witnessed others perform have done it or seen others do. But, this is something you can discover

at your own risk. You must be aware is that the results cannot be certain, and it might be straightforward to

Some people, it could be more difficult for some people than for.

This book is crucial for those who have thought of giving telekinesis a test. It is essential to note that it is not necessary.

not to make the necessary preparations to ensure this happens. If you follow the guidelines given here

And if you do different exercises by the instructor, you significantly increase the chances of success

in telekinesis.

Before you start your journey, it is important be ready to accept the reality that it's not simple and it will be a long haul.

involves lots of effort perseverance, commitment, and dedication. There is the slightest possibility

You can harness using your brain's ability to control objects in your environment, why wouldn't you?

What are you waiting for? It's a chance to fully explore your potential And you never know. You could be among the very few people have the ability to accomplish this. If it is,

If you'd like to test it out , then good luck. If you don't, then you could share this information with others

Around you as you never know who it could have an interest for.